Company Secretarial Checklists

Company Secretarial Checklists

Douglas Armour ACIS

Partner
David Venus & Company

ICSA Publishing
The Official Publishing Company of
The Institute of Chartered Secretaries and Administrators

First published 1992 by
ICSA Publishing Limited
Campus 400
Maylands Avenue
Hemel Hempstead
Hertfordshire, HP2 7EZ

Copyright © ICSA Publishing 1992

All rights reserved. No part of this publication may be reproduced, stored in a retrieval system, or transmitted, in any form, or by any means, electronic, mechanical, photocopying, recording or otherwise, without prior permission, in writing, from the publisher.

Typeset in 10/12pt Meridien
by Hands Fotoset, Leicester

Printed and bound in Great Britain by
BPCC Wheatons Ltd, Exeter

British Library Cataloguing in Publication Data

A catalogue record for this book is available from the British Library

ISBN 1-872860-14-1

1 2 3 4 5   96 95 94 93 92

Contents

Preface	vii
Accounting reference date	1
Accounts – approval	3
– dormant companies	5
– late filing penalties	7
Acquisition of non-cash assets	8
Agreement to short notice	10
Annual General Meeting	11
Annual Returns	14
Articles of Association (adoption or change)	15
Audited accounts – modified	17
Auditors – appointment	20
– removal	22
– resignation	24
Authorised share capital – increase	26
Bank account	28
Bonus Issue (Capitalisation Issue)	30
Borrowing powers	32
Business names	33
Calls	34
Debenture stock	36
Directors – appointment	37
– ceasing to hold office	39
– duties	42
– meetings	45
– removal	47
Dissolution	49
Dividends	51
Documents – retention periods	53
Dormant companies	57
Elective Resolutions	59
Extraordinary General Meetings	61
Extraordinary General Meetings – requisition	62
Forfeiture	64
Headed paper	66

CONTENTS

Incorporation	68
Incorporation – first board meeting	70
Joint shareholders	72
Joint shareholders – death of one holder	73
Loan stock	74
Loan stock – conversion	76
– unsecured	78
Memorandum of Association	80
Name change	81
Notices	83
Pre-emption rights – allotment	84
– transfer	86
Purchase of own shares	88
Purchase of own shares – financial assistance	90
Redemptions and purchases out of capital	92
Register of Members – rectification	94
Re-registration of a limited company as unlimited	95
Re-registration of a private company as a public limited company	97
Re-registration of a public limited company as a private limited company	100
Re-registration of an unlimited company as a limited company	102
Re-registration of other companies as public companies	104
Related party transactions	106
Resolutions – filing requirements	108
– majority	110
Resolutions in writing	111
Restoration	114
Rights Issue	116
Secretary – appointment	118
– duties	120
Sensitive words	122
Share Certificate – duplicate	130
Shareholders – Power of Attorney	131
– Probate	133
Shares – application and allotment	135
– consolidation	137
– convertible	139
– cumulative	141
– redeemable	143
– transfer	144
Single member companies	146
Statutory forms and filing periods	148
Statutory registers	155

Preface

This book has been written as a handy quick-reference guide to the more common company secretarial procedures. It is not intended to be a legal reference book and accordingly little explanation of relevant legislation is made. On points of complexity reference should be made to specialist books or to the legislation itself.

The procedures and notes for each topic should not be regarded as an exhaustive list of the procedures to be followed in all circumstances. The procedures are a guide to the reader indicating procedures that should be considered in the context of the particular company in question.

The checklists have been compiled with the private company in mind, although many of the procedures are equally suitable to both private and public companies.

Although the book will be a useful addition to any business bookshelf, it will be of particular interest to the following:

- *Accountants/auditors.* Many private company directors will turn to their accountant for advice on company secretarial matters. This book sets out answers to the majority of questions likely to be asked.
- *Solicitors/chartered secretary practices.* Whilst most solicitors and chartered secretaries will have legal reference and textbooks these are often too detailed for quick reference. This book will complement rather than duplicate existing reference sources.
- *Company secretaries/directors.* Even where advice will be sought from their professional advisers, all company secretaries should find the book useful when advising their directors. An understanding of the procedures involved for any particular matter will facilitate proper discussion at board level, collation of relevant information and the giving of instructions to professional advisers.

Having worked in public practice for over seven years, the author has included those practical points and procedures that company secretaries and practitioners will find most useful.

The author would like to thank his partner, David Venus, for his practical advice and proofreading skills, and Enid Birchall for typing the manuscript.

Whilst every effort has been made to ensure the accuracy of the content of this book, neither the author nor the publisher can accept responsibility for any loss arising to anyone relying on the information contained herein.

Douglas Armour

Accounting reference date

Procedure

1. The directors must authorise the change in accounting year end at a board meeting.
2. Form G225(1) or G225(2) must be filed with the Registrar of Companies.

Notes

The first accounting period must be longer than six months but not more than eighteen months from the date of incorporation.

Subsequent periods may not be longer than eighteen months but may be as short as the company wishes.

A new company has nine months from the date of incorporation in which to notify its accounting reference date to the Registrar of Companies. If a new company does not notify an accounting reference date within that time it will be given as its accounting reference date the last day of the anniversary of the month of its incorporation.

A company can only extend its accounting year once in any five-year period unless it is being changed to be brought into line with that of its holding company or any subsidiary. The accounting period can be shortened as many times as required.

3. Notification of the change in year end must be made to the Registrar of Companies. Unless the change is being made to bring the company's accounting period into line with that of a holding company or subsidiary, the change of accounting period can only be made during the accounting period. It is not possible to change the length of an accounting period that has already ended. The change in

2 COMPANY SECRETARIAL CHECKLISTS

year end will only become effective once the appropriate form has been received by the Registrar of Companies.
4. If extending the accounting period, the directors must first check that the accounting year end has not already been extended in the previous five years.

Notes

The date by which accounts must be submitted to the Registrar may be shortened when the accounting period is for a period less than twelve months (see page 4).

In addition to notifying the Registrar of Companies, the directors may also consider notifying the following:

> Bankers, auditors, accountants, Inland Revenue, subsidiaries, joint venture partners, VAT Office.

Companies House requirements

- G224, G225(1) or G225(2) as appropriate.

References

The Companies Act 1985 S224, S225.

Accounts – approval

Audited accounts are approved by the Board of Directors and issued to the shareholders.

Although the shareholders consider and receive the accounts and can vote on whether or not to accept them, they do not, strictly speaking, approve them. If rejected by the shareholders, the Directors are not obliged to amend the accounts unless they contain a factual error. However, in such circumstances non-acceptance of accounts will be regarded as a vote of no confidence in the Board.

Procedure

1. Final draft of the accounts to be approved by the directors.
2. The Directors' Report and the Balance Sheet must be signed. The Directors' Report should be signed by the secretary or a director, the Balance Sheet *must* be signed by at least one director. The published accounts must have the names of the director and/or secretary who have signed the Balance Sheet and Directors' Report typed thereon.
3. It is possible for one director to sign both the Directors' Report and the Balance Sheet.
4. Signed copies of the accounts must be returned to the auditors so that the Audit Report can be signed.
5. One signed copy of the accounts must be filed with the Registrar of Companies within the appropriate period (see paragraph 10 below).
6. Copies of the accounts must be sent to the shareholders and a meeting of the shareholders convened, for the shareholders to consider the accounts, within ten months of the year end for a private company (seven for public).

3

4 COMPANY SECRETARIAL CHECKLISTS

7. Certain companies are able to file modified accounts with the Registrar of Companies (see page 17).
8. Full accounts will be required for issue to the shareholders and to the Inland Revenue.
9. Additional copies will normally be sent to the company's bankers.
10. The period for delivery of accounts to the Registrar is ten months from the end of the accounting period for a private company and seven months for a public company unless:
    (a) If the accounts are the first accounts and are for a period in excess of twelve months, the accounts must be submitted no later than ten months from the first anniversary of incorporation or three months from the end of the period, whichever expires last.
    (b) Where the accounting period has been shortened the period for delivery of the accounts shall be ten months for private companies or seven months for public companies from the end of the period or three months from the date of notice, whichever expires last.

The Registrar of Companies imposes penalties for late submission of accounts and when setting the accounting reference date, care must be taken to ensure that the accounts can be prepared with sufficient time to submit them to the Registrar of Companies. (See page 7.)

The forms required to notify a change in year end to the Registrar of Companies are forms G224, G225(1) and G225(2), as the case may be.

Companies House requirements

- Copy of accounts normally within ten or seven months as appropriate.
- Accounts must have original signatures on Directors' Report, Audit Report and Balance Sheet.
- Name of person signing must be shown.
- Company registration number must be shown on first page.
- As the Registrar will unbind and discard any folder, it is best to file an unbound copy of the accounts.

References

The Companies Act 1985 S233, S234A, S235, S236, S238, S241, S242, S244.

Accounts – dormant companies

Where a company has not traded during any particular financial year, the company can dispense with the obligation to prepare audited accounts.

Procedure

1. If the company has been dormant since its incorporation, a Special Resolution exempting the company from the obligation to appoint auditors must be approved prior to any general meeting convened to consider the accounts.
2. Where the company becomes dormant during any financial year, the relevant resolution must be approved at the general meeting convened to consider the last 'trading' accounts.
3. In both cases the Board of Directors must convene a general meeting of the shareholders, of which at least twenty-one clear days' notice is required.
4. The meeting may, however, be held upon short notice.
5. If approved at the meeting, a copy of the resolution must be filed with the Registrar of Companies within fifteen days.
6. Non-trading, non-audited accounts must be prepared and filed with the Registrar in the normal manner.
7. The non-audited accounts must contain a statement immediately above the signature(s) of the director(s) on the Balance Sheet to the effect that the company was dormant throughout the year.

Notes

The Special Resolution remains in force until such time as the company no longer qualifies as a dormant company. In these circumstances the

6 COMPANY SECRETARIAL CHECKLISTS

directors must appoint auditors. There is no requirement to notify Companies House of the change in status of the company.

To remain as dormant, any costs must be paid by the directors or shareholders personally or by a holding company. In particular the company must not pay its own Annual Return filing fee.

Companies House requirements

- Copy of Special Resolution.
- Copy of non-trading, non-audited accounts – annually.

References

The Companies Act 1985 S250.

Accounts – late filing penalties

Under provisions introduced under the Companies Act 1989, if accounts – whether audited or dormant – are received by the Registrar of Companies once the due date is passed, then the company will be fined automatically according to a sliding scale.

It should be noted that the onus on directors is to *deliver* accounts to the Registrar of Companies within the time-scales, not simply to *post* them within the time-scales. Late filing penalties do not apply to Annual Returns.

The scale of penalties is as follows:

	Private companies	Public companies
Up to 3 months late	£100	£500
Up to 6 months late	£250	£1,000
Up to 12 months late	£500	£2,000
More than 12 months late	£1,000	£5,000

Notes

The penalties are imposed on the company, not the directors, and are a civil matter.

It should also be noted that under certain circumstances the directors may also be prosecuted for failure to submit accounts on time, which is a criminal offence, and on conviction a maximum fine of £2,000 may be imposed by the court for each separate offence.

References

The Companies Act 1985 S242, S242A.

Acquisition of non-cash assets

Where a public company proposes to acquire non-cash assets from its subscribers, or in the circumstances where a private company is re-registered as a public company and the company wishes to acquire certain non-cash assets from the members of the company at that time or within a period of two years from the re-registration, special requirements apply.

During this period the company may only acquire non-cash assets from its members if the following procedure is followed.

Transactions involving assets with an aggregate value representing less than 10 per cent in nominal value of the company's issued share capital are exempt from these requirements.

Procedure

1. The asset to be acquired by the company must be valued by an independent valuer and a written report made within six months of the proposed acquisition.
2. The terms of the proposed acquisition together with a copy of the valuer's report must be approved by Ordinary Resolution of the members.
3. If the person from whom the assets are to be acquired is no longer a member of the company but was at the time of re-registration or was a subscriber of the company, a copy of the notice and the resolutions and Report must be circulated to them as well.
4. The report by the independent valuer must confirm that on the basis of their valuation the consideration to be received by the company is not less than the value of the consideration being paid (i.e. cash or shares).
5. A signed copy of the Ordinary Resolution approving the acquisition must be submitted to the Registrar of Companies within fifteen days of its approval.

ACQUISITION OF NON-CASH ASSETS

6. The above provisions will apply even where the acquisition is only in part the acquisition of non-cash assets, provided that they exceed 10 per cent in nominal value of the company's issued share capital.

Notes

Where these provisions have not been followed, the company is entitled to reclaim any consideration paid to its subscribers or members and the agreement shall be void.

If the consideration paid by the company is the allotment of shares credited as fully paid, the company shall be entitled to request from the allottee an amount equal to the nominal value of the shares together with any share premium.

References

The Companies Act 1985 S104, S105.

Agreement to short notice

It is possible for shareholders in most instances to agree to accept shorter notice of a meeting than that prescribed by the Companies Act.

For short notice of an Annual General Meeting it is necessary for all the members to agree.

For any other meeting members holding at least 95 per cent of the voting shares must agree to the meeting being held at short notice. This level of 95 per cent can be reduced to 90 per cent by a prior Elective Resolution which itself will require 100 per cent approval.

It is not necessary for all the members to attend the meeting, simply that they agree to the short notice being given.

The Agreement to Short Notice must be given in writing and the agreement(s) should be inserted in the company's Minute Book along with the relevant minutes.

In the circumstances where the meeting being convened is to consider the company's audited accounts, it is also necessary for the members to agree to the accounts being received less than twenty-one days before the meeting.

Although certain resolutions require that special notice be given, the calling of the meeting upon short notice will not in itself invalidate the resolution. However, caution must be taken when calling upon short notice meetings of which special notice has been given.

Certain resolutions (i.e. financial assistance) require that documents be made available for inspection for a set period prior to the meeting. Accordingly, the ability to convene the appropriate meeting upon short notice is limited.

References

The Companies Act 1985 S369.

Annual General Meeting

Unless the company has adopted the elective regime (see page 59), it is necessary for all companies to hold an Annual General Meeting (AGM), in each calendar year and not more than fifteen months since the previous one.

The company's first AGM must be held within eighteen months of its incorporation.

The normal or 'ordinary' business of the AGM is to consider the latest accounts, confirm the declaration of a final dividend (where appropriate), approve the remuneration of the directors and the auditors, and to re-elect the auditors and retiring directors, if necessary. Any other business is deemed to be 'special' business.

Procedure

1. The directors will decide on the date of the AGM, formally approve any accounts to be considered by the meeting, declare any final dividend payable and authorise the secretary to issue a notice to the shareholders.
2. The notice must be issued to the members not less than twenty-one clear days before the meeting. 'Clear days' exclude the days of issue and receipt. Receipt will normally be deemed to be the day following the day of posting but sometimes the Articles of Association will stipulate that the day of receipt is two days after posting. The Articles should be consulted to ascertain the particular provisions.
3. Companies with a large number of members and those with outside shareholders should enclose proxy forms with the notice, although this is not a requirement. It should be noted, however, that where proxy forms are to be issued with the notice they must be issued to *all* the shareholders and not just to a selected few.

12   COMPANY SECRETARIAL CHECKLISTS

4. The secretary should arrange for a suitable venue for the meeting.
5. A copy of the notice should also be sent to the directors and to the auditors. If the AGM is to consider the accounts, these should be issued with the notice.
6. Before the meeting the secretary should check and count all the proxies received.
7. At the meeting the secretary should ensure that an attendance sheet is circulated.
8. Preferably arrangements should be made to ensure that shareholders alone have access to the meeting; however, this is not always possible or desirable in practice.
9. At the meeting, unless waived by the meeting, the notice, the Directors' Report and the Audit Report should be read to the meeting.

Notes

There is no longer a statutory requirement for the Audit Report to be read to the meeting. If present, the auditor will usually read the Audit Report.

If the meeting is being held at short notice and the accounts are to be considered, the members must also agree to receive the accounts at short notice. For companies with a large number of shareholders, or at meetings where there may be questions from the floor, it is useful to prepare a chairman's script prior to the meeting. Additionally, the directors should meet prior to the meeting to discuss any matters that might be raised at the meeting and to decide which of them will deal with certain queries.

If a poll is likely, the secretary should arrange for poll cards to be available. Companies who use registrars will normally use their services when conducting a poll.

Additional copies of the latest audited accounts and directors' service contracts must be available at the meeting, together with a copy of the Register of Members, minutes of previous meetings of the shareholders and the Registers of Directors, Directors' Interests and copies of directors' service contracts.

If it is likely that a poll will be required for any resolution, the directors should ensure that as many proxy forms are received prior to the meeting as possible. It is important that proxy forms are received at the Registered Office or the office of the registrars forty-eight hours before the meeting – otherwise they cannot be accepted. Any proxy forms brought to the meeting are invalid.

References

The Companies Act 1985 S366, S366A, S369.

Annual Returns

The company is required to file an Annual Return in respect of each calendar year made up to a date not more than twelve months from the date of the previous Annual Return.

The Annual Return must be filed within twenty-eight days of its made-up date.

Although Annual Returns will be accepted for filing outside the 28-day period, where the Return has been made to a date prior to its existing Return date then this Return date will remain unaltered. In such circumstances a second Return will be due made up to the Return date.

The majority of companies will receive a 'shuttle' form of the Annual Return issued by Companies House. This shuttle document contains pre-printed details of the company's Registered Office, trade classification, secretary and directors. Any changes to the information shown can be added to the form. Additionally, details of the company's issued share capital, and any of the directors' additional directorships must be completed each year. Details of the shareholders need only be given once every three years if there have been no changes. Where there have been changes details of the changes only may be given, provided that a full list is submitted once every three years.

An Annual Return cannot be submitted to Companies House prior to its made-up date.

References

The Companies Act 1985 S363, S364, S364A, S365.

Articles of Association
(adoption or change)

The articles of Association of a company are the rules governing its internal affairs. Table A of the Companies Act 1985 contains a model set of articles. However, most registration agents have their own variation and as a result few companies are incorporated solely with Table A as their articles.

Alteration of any particular regulation or adoption of new articles requires a Special Resolution of the members in general meeting.

Procedure

1. Directors should formally convene a meeting of the shareholders and decide upon a date and venue for the meeting. They will also authorise the secretary to issue a notice to the shareholders. The notice will contain the wording of the new clauses or, where new articles are to be adopted, a copy of the articles should be enclosed with the notice.
2. If the meeting is to be convened upon short notice, the secretary should arrange for Agreement to Short Notice to be signed by each of the shareholders.
3. If the share capital of the company is divided into more than one class, it may be necessary for separate class meetings to be held in addition to the general meeting.
4. At the general meeting (or class meetings) the resolutions will require a 75 per cent majority of those present in person or by proxy.
5. If passed, a copy of the resolution must be submitted to the Registrar of Companies within fifteen days. In addition, an amended copy of the Articles of Association should be submitted to the Registrar of Companies.

Notes

Although it is not necessary to issue new copies of the Memorandum and Articles of Association to the shareholders, the company should ensure that it has a supply for issue to those shareholders who request a copy. In addition, a copy will normally be sent to the company's bankers and to their auditors.

Companies House requirements

- A signed copy of the resolution within fifteen days.
- Amended copy of the Articles within fifteen days.

References

The Companies Act 1985 S9, S18, S19.

Audited accounts – modified

Certain smaller companies qualifying as either small or medium-sized may file modified accounts with the Registrar of Companies. In order to qualify as a medium-sized company in respect of any particular financial year, the company must be or have been medium-sized during one or more of the following periods:

1. Since incorporation;
2. In that year and in the year before;
3. In the two years before that year; or
4. In that year and in any two of the preceding three years.

A medium-sized company is one which meets any two of the following requirements:

1. Turnover not exceeding £8 million.
2. Balance Sheet total not exceeding £3.9 million.
3. Average number of employees not exceeding 250.

The information required for modified accounts of a medium-sized company is:

1. Full Balance Sheet.
2. Profit and Loss Account.
3. Special Auditors' Report.
4. Directors' Report.

Additionally there must be the following notes to the accounts:

1. A statement above the director's signature on the Balance Sheet that the director's accounts have relied on the exemptions for individual

accounts on the grounds that the company is entitled to benefit from those exemptions as a medium-sized company.
2. The special Auditors' Report should state that the requirements for exemption are satisfied and reproduce the Auditors' Report from the full accounts.
3. The Profit and Loss Account may be abbreviated and need not disclose turnover.

In order to qualify as a small company in respect of any particular financial year, the company must have been small-sized during one or more of the following periods:

1. Since incorporation;
2. In that year and the year before;
3. In the two years before that year; or
4. In that year and in any two of the preceding three years.

A small-sized company must meet any two of the following criteria:

1. Turnover not exceeding £2 million.
2. Balance Sheet total not exceeding £975,000.
3. Average number of employees not exceeding fifty.

Modified accounts of a small-sized company must contain the following information:

1. Abbreviated version of the full Balance Sheet.
2. Special Auditors' Report.

Additionally there must be the following notes to the accounts:

1. A statement above the director's signature on the Balance Sheet that the director's accounts have relied on the exemptions for individual accounts on the grounds that the company is entitled to benefit from those exemptions as a small-sized company.
2. The special Auditors' Report should state that the requirements for exemption are satisfied and reproduce the Auditors' Report from the full accounts.

Notes

It must be noted that although modified accounts can be submitted to

AUDITED ACCOUNTS – MODIFIED 19

the Registrar and thus reduce the amount of information on public file, it is still necessary to produce full accounts for circulation to the company's shareholders and for submission to the Inland Revenue. Accordingly the preparation of modified accounts may result in additional work for the auditors and cost to the company.

References

The Companies Act 1985 S246, S247, S248, S249.

Auditors – appointment

All companies that have not resolved not to appoint auditors (see page 5) must prepare audited accounts.

The company's first auditors will be appointed by the directors and must be appointed at any time before the first general meeting at which accounts are laid before the shareholders.

Auditors are only appointed to act until the conclusion of the next general meeting at which accounts are laid before the shareholders. Private companies can elect not to re-appoint auditors annually by an elective resolution. In such circumstances the auditors are deemed to be re-appointed for each succeeding financial year until such time as either the company becomes dormant or a resolution to the effect that the auditors' appointment be brought to an end is passed.

In such circumstances where the auditors have resigned or been removed during the year, the directors may appoint auditors to fill this casual vacancy. However, at the next general meeting at which accounts are considered, a Special Notice is required for the resolution to re-appoint the new auditors. In addition, it is a requirement that the old auditors be given notice of this resolution.

An auditor is required to be registered as an auditor, and must not be an officer or a servant of the company or partners or employees of such officers or servants. An auditor may be an individual, a partnership or a limited company.

Notes

The directors must check the auditors' qualification to act.

The company may wish to notify its bankers, solicitors, subsidiaries, etc. of the auditors' appointment.

References

The Companies Act 1989 S25–S54 (inclusive).
The Companies Act 1985 S384–S388A (inclusive).

Auditors – removal

Procedure

Where it is decided to remove auditors from office, the following procedure should be maintained:

1. Special Notice of the proposed resolution must be given by a member to the company.
2. The directors are not obliged to convene the meeting and the member(s) may have to requisition the meeting (see page 62).
3. Once the Special Notice has been received, copies must be sent by the company to the auditors who are to be removed and, if relevant, to the persons to be appointed as auditors in their place, if this is to be done at the same meeting.
4. The auditors to be removed may make representations in writing to the company and may request that such representations be circulated to the members. The company is obliged to circulate the statements or, in the event that they are received with insufficient time before the meeting, they must be read to the meeting. If it appears that the auditors are making false representations or defamatory statements, the company may apply to the court to be relieved of this obligation.
5. The auditor who is being removed is entitled to receive notice of and to attend and speak at the general meeting.
6. Once the resolution removing the auditor has been passed, the company must notify the removed auditors in writing of this fact and must file a copy with the Registrar of Companies.

Companies House requirements

- Copy of notice removing auditors within fourteen days.

References

The Companies Act 1985 S391, S391A.

Auditors – resignation

Auditors may resign from office by giving notice in writing to the Registered Office of the company and a copy must be filed with the Registrar of Companies. The notice must be accompanied by a statement that there are no circumstances connected with their resignation that should be brought to the notice of members or creditors or, alternatively, that there *are* circumstances to be brought to their attention and a statement of those circumstances must be enclosed.

Procedure

1. Within twenty-eight days of depositing their statement with the company, the auditors must file a copy with the Registrar of Companies.
2. Within fourteen days of receipt of the statement, the company must circulate copies of the statement to the shareholders and directors and any other persons who would normally receive copies of the company's audited accounts.
3. Alternatively, the company may apply to the court within fourteen days to restrain publication of the statement.
4. The resigning auditors may require that a general meeting be convened to consider the reasons for their resignation and that a statement be circulated to the shareholders. The company may, however, apply to the court to relieve the company from this obligation if the resigning auditors are using this procedure for defamatory or improper purposes.

Companies House requirements

- Copy of letter of resignation.
- Copy of statement setting out reasons for resignation, if appropriate.

References

The Companies Act 1985 S392, S392A.

Authorised share capital – increase

The Articles of Association normally allow the members of the company by Ordinary Resolution to increase the company's authorised share capital.

Procedure

1. At a meeting of the Board of Directors the directors should convene an Extraordinary General Meeting to increase the authorised share capital whether by increasing the number of shares of existing classes or by the creation of a new class or classes of shares.
2. Where the increase in capital is by the creation of a new class of shares, it will be necessary to introduce regulations to the Articles of Association setting out the rules governing the shares, and these amendments will need to be made by Special Resolution.
3. The notice convening the Extraordinary General Meeting must be made upon fourteen days' clear notice for any Ordinary Resolutions or upon twenty-one clear days' notice where Special Resolutions are to be approved. Alternatively, a meeting may be convened upon short notice provided at least 95 per cent of the members agree.
4. If approved, a copy of the resolutions must be submitted to the Registrar of Companies within fifteen days, together with a Notice of Increase in Nominal Capital on form G123.
5. A copy of the resolutions should be attached to all copies of the memorandum and Articles of Association by the company and any further copies to be printed should be amended to show the increased capital.

AUTHORISED SHARE CAPITAL – INCREASE 27

Notes

When the authorised share capital is increased an ordinary resolution to confer authority upon the directors to allot the new shares should also be approved. In addition it may be necessary or appropriate to seek approval for a special resolution to waive any rights of pre-emption on allotment (see page 84) (S.80 Companies Act 1985).

Companies House requirements

- Copy of Ordinary Resolution(s)
- Copy of any Special Resolution (if required).
- Form G123.

References

The Companies Act 1985 S121, S122, S123.

Bank account

The operation of a bank account and banking matters generally are controlled by the Board of Directors.

All banks have a standard form of Mandate and these are usually in the form of draft minutes. Once the text of the authority and the instructions have been approved by the board, a signed copy of the Mandate should be inserted in the company's Minute Book as evidence of the appropriate decisions being reached.

The majority of banks will require security or collateral for overdraft facilities and care must be taken to ensure that the directors have authority to charge the company's assets.

Procedure

1. The directors must authorise the opening and operation of a bank account at a Board meeting.
2. The company secretary will normally complete the bank Mandate form as directed by the directors, and the Mandate, a copy of the company's up-to-date Memorandum and Articles of Association and the original Certificate of Incorporation (and any Certificates of Incorporation on Change of Name) must be submitted to the bank. The bank will note and return the original Certificates of Incorporation.
3. Care must be taken to ensure that the signatories required for cheques are reasonable in the circumstances. Often companies will empower an authorised signatory to sign cheques up to a certain sum limit, with directors – often two – required to sign cheques of larger amounts.
4. The frequency that the company receive bank statements should also be chosen.

5. The banks prefer the Mandate to be expressed in terms of the position held by the signatories rather than their specific names. If a named person is shown, when that person leaves the company it is necessary to complete a new Mandate rather than just merely changing the signatory.

Notes

It is normal practice to inform the bank when directors, secretary, the Registered Office, the company's accounting reference date or the company's auditors change.

The bank will often require a copy of the company's latest audited accounts for their records.

Bonus Issue (Capitalisation Issue)

A Bonus or Capitalisation Issue is one by which the company allots shares that are partly or fully paid and no further payment from the shareholder is normally required. If the bonus shares are partly paid, the unpaid portion may be called at some future date.

The company's capacity to issue partly or fully paid shares will be contained in the company's Articles of Association but in any event will also require approval of the shareholders by Ordinary Resolution. Although a Capitalisation or Bonus Issue is an issue of new shares, no new capital is raised and it is effected by capitalising some or all of the company's distributable reserves.

There are a number of reasons why companies may wish to issue shares in this manner, the more common ones being: to increase the company's issued share capital in order to re-register as a public company without requiring the shareholders to inject further funds; to declare a Bonus Issue in conjunction with a Rights Issue to reduce the potential dilution of the holdings of those shareholders who do not take up any shares under the offer; or to create a more meaningful Balance Sheet by capitalising reserves into issued share capital.

Procedure

1. The Articles of Association must be checked to ensure that the company has power to effect a capitalisation of its distributable reserves and to ensure that the company has sufficient authorised but unissued share capital.
2. The directors must be authorised in terms of Section 80 of the Companies Act 1985 to allot shares. The directors should convene a general meeting of the shareholders to authorise the directors to effect the Bonus or Capitalisation Issue by Ordinary Resolution and

BONUS ISSUE (CAPITALISATION ISSUE)

in addition to increase the directors' authority to allot shares, and where appropriate to increase the company's authorised share capital and to authorise the company to capitalise its reserves as the case may be.
3. As bonus shares are issued pro-rata, it should not be necessary to waive any rights of pre-emption, unless the members have the option to renounce their entitlement.
4. Copies of the appropriate resolutions must be filed with the Registrar of Companies within fifteen days.
5. Once the resolutions have been passed, the secretary should issue Letters of Allotment or Renounceable Letters of Allotment, as the case may be, to the shareholders. Renounceable Letters of Allotment would be used to enable shareholders to renounce their rights in favour of some other person.
6. On expiration of the renunciation period Share Certificates should be prepared and the directors should authorise the issue of certificates.
7. Share Certificates should be despatched to the allottees as soon as practicable and in any event within two months of the date of issue of the shares.
8. The appropriate Form of Allotment should be submitted to the Registrar of Companies on form G88(2), together with a copy of the written agreement to capitalise the reserves or form G88(3), as appropriate.
9. The secretary should ensure that the Register of Members is amended to show the additional shares being issued.

Notes

On completion of the Bonus or Capitalisation Issue it will be necessary to inform the company's accountants, both internal and external, so that the appropriate entries to the company's accounts can be made.

Companies House requirements

- Copies of any Ordinary or Special Resolutions.
- Forms G123, G88(2), G88(3).

References

The Companies Act 1985 S88, S185, S263.

Borrowing powers

No company incorporated under the Companies Act 1985 and incorporating Table A without amendment will have specific authority in its Articles for the directors to exercise the company's borrowing capacity. Table A assumes that directors have full authority to exercise the company's borrowing powers, unless such power is specifically limited in the Articles.

Accordingly, companies incorporated under the Companies Act 1985 will have the borrowing capacity contained in the company's Memorandum of Association together with any limitations set out in the Articles. Companies incorporated under previous Companies Acts only have a limited borrowing power contained in the Articles unless this authority contained in the 'old' Table A has been amended in the Articles or by subsequent resolution.

If the directors' capacity to exercise the company's borrowing power is not sufficient for their purposes, it will be necessary for the Articles of Association to be amended by Special Resolution (see page 15).

Business names

A business name is a name or title by which a company may trade other than its corporate or registered name.

There is no longer a register of business names.

The headed paper of a company using a business name must show the company name in full as well as the business name, in addition to the other statutory requirements (see page 66).

The name of the proprietor must be shown at all business premises.

Companies using business names must take care so as not to infringe registered names, trade marks or pass themselves off as other registered companies, partnerships or sole traders.

References

The Company and Business Names Regulations 1981.
The Companies Act 1985 S349.
The Business Names Act 1985 S4.

Calls

Where, for any reason, shares have been issued as partly paid, the amounts unpaid can be called by the directors at any time either in full or in part.

The liability for the unpaid amounts rests with the registered holder.

The company should not accept registration of a transfer of shares upon which there remains an unpaid call unless the transferee is willing to pay the unpaid call.

Procedure

1. The directors should pass a resolution to make the call at a Board meeting. The resolution should detail the amounts to be called and the date upon which the call is being made.
2. The secretary should arrange the preparation and issue of call letters to each shareholder. Each letter should be addressed to the registered holder or joint holders, as the case may be, and should contain details of the registered shareholders(s), the amounts currently outstanding and the amount now being called, together with details of when the payment is due.
3. Each call letter should carry a distinguishing number and this number should be noted on the Register of Members together with a note of the amount being called. The company should compile lists of the payments as they are received and cleared by the bank. Once the date on which the call is due has passed, the list of payments should be reconciled with the Register of Members and a list of unpaid calls should be prepared.
4. A reminder letter should be sent to all shareholders who have not paid the call, requesting immediate payment and warning of the potential penalties for non-payment of the call, including forfeiture of shares or suspension of voting rights.

5. Shareholders should return their Share Certificates together with a copy of the call letter so that the Share Certificates may be endorsed by the company, giving details of the paid call. The endorsed Share Certificate should be returned to the shareholder.
6. The Register of Members should be amended to include details of the additional amounts now paid on the shares.

Notes

Where calls remain unpaid, there are a number of actions the directors can take, although the Articles of Association should be checked to ensure that the directors have the requisite authority.

The directors may institute proceedings for the forfeiture of the shares, under which circumstances the shares are forfeited by the holder and cancelled or re-issued. In the instance of re-issue the company should return to the shareholders the amounts paid by them on the shares. The Articles of Association may authorise the directors to withhold any dividends from the shareholder and credit these amounts to the share capital account until such time as the call has been paid.

Alternatively, the shareholder may lose the right to vote until such time as the call has been paid.

It will be necessary to inform the company's auditors of the call and the split between the calls that were paid and any unpaid calls. Occasionally shares will be issued as partly paid with the balance payable on fixed instalment dates. The procedure to be followed in such circumstances is the same as that for making a call.

References

The Companies (Tables A to F) Regulations 1985, Table A Regulations 12–22.

Debenture stock

The procedures for issuing, transferring, payment of interest on and redemption of debentures are broadly speaking the same as for the issuing of Ordinary Shares.

The regulations governing the issue of debentures and any rights and privileges attaching to the debentures are contained in a Trust Deed. The Trust Deed will usually include the following matters:

Details of the stock, terms of issue, payment of interest, conversion into shares and/or redemption.

Provisions constituting charges over the assets of the company in favour of the Trust Deed and giving details of the events by which the charge would be enforceable.

Details of the Trustees' powers to concur with the company in dealings with the charged assets.

Where the security is by way of floating charge, a prohibition on the company issuing any further security ranking in priority to the debenture stock without previous consent.

Details setting out the form of stock certificate, conditions of redemption, conversion rights and regulations in respect of the Register of Holders, transfer and transmission, and regulations for the conducting and holding of meetings of the debenture holders.

References

The Companies Act 1985 S190–S197 (inclusive).

Directors – appointment

When a company is incorporated, the people named in the incorporation papers (form G10) as directors and who have consented to act are deemed to be appointed on the date of incorporation. Following the appointment of these first directors, any further directors to be appointed should be appointed in accordance with the regulations laid down by the company's Articles of Association.

In general the Articles will allow the existing directors to fill any casual vacancy in their number by themselves or by the shareholders in general meeting.

Occasionally the Articles of Association will stipulate qualifications to be held for eligibility for appointment as a director. In previous years this would often be a share qualification, although this is no longer a popular practice. Additional qualifications would more normally be the holding of a particular professional or technical qualification (e.g. chartered surveyor, architect, etc.).

Procedure for appointment

1. The Board of Directors should formally appoint the new director. Alternatively a director may be appointed by the members in general meeting.
2. The new director should complete and sign a form G288 containing details of their full name, residential address, date of birth, nationality, business occupation and details of any other UK directorships held during the previous five years.
    The form G288 should be submitted to the Registrar of Companies within fourteen days of the appointment.
3. The director's details should be included in the company's Register of Directors and any interest in shares inserted in the Register of Directors' Interests.

4. The company's bankers should be informed and the bank Mandate amended if required.
5. The new director should notify the Board of any interest in contracts or other companies with which the company has dealings
6. The secretary should inform the new director of the dates upon which forthcoming Board meetings are to be held, if known.
7. If the directors' names are shown on the company's headed stationery, the details of the new director should be inserted.
8. The appointment of the new director can be notified to staff and/or customers if desired. Larger companies may issue a press release.
9. If the Articles of Association require that the directors hold a share qualification, it is essential that the director acquires the appropriate shares within two months or the time limit set down by the Articles if shorter.
10. If the new director is to be an executive director, it may be considered necessary for the director to have a formal service contract with the company.
11. It may be necessary to add the director to the company's Directors' Indemnity Insurance Policy or indeed it may be necessary to effect such a policy.
12. If this is the director's first appointment as director, he should be given guidance as to his duties and responsibilities in terms of the Companies Act and his fiduciary responsibility to the shareholders.
13. The Inland Revenue should be informed of the director's appointment.

Companies House requirements

- Form G288.

References

The Companies Act 1985 S10, S282, S284, S288, S289, S291–S294, S305, S310, S317.

Directors – ceasing to hold office

A director may cease to hold office in a number of ways, including death, by statute and under the provisions of the Articles of Association.

A director may be barred from holding or continuing to hold office as director for the following reasons:

1. If the Articles require that the director hold a share qualification and the director does not acquire the necessary shares within two months or the time limit specified by the Articles if shorter.
2. If the director reaches the relevant age limit for directors stipulated in the Articles of Association.
3. If the director becomes bankrupt (unless permitted by the court).
4. If the director is disqualified from holding a directorship by a Court Order.

Additionally, the Articles may stipulate certain events which will require the director to vacate office, including:

5. If a director resigns – resignation will not normally require consent of the remaining directors, although this may be required by the Articles.
6. If a director is absent from Board meetings for a specific period without authority of the Board.
7. If a director has a Receiving Order made against him or if he enters into arrangements with his creditors.
8. If the director is, or may be, suffering from a mental disorder and either the director has been admitted to hospital pursuant to the Mental Health Act or a Court Order has been made requiring his detention under the Act.
9. If a director is removed from office by the remaining directors or by the shareholders in some specified manner. This may include

Written Resolution of the remaining directors, by notice in writing of the company's holding company or in certain circumstances by their appointer. (For example, the holders of a particular class of shares may have the right to appoint a director and this person may be removed by them.)
10. In addition to these powers contained in the Articles of Association or by statute, the shareholders of the company have the right at all times to remove a director by Ordinary Resolution. Care must be taken when using these provisions and they are dealt with in more detail on page 47.

Procedure on a director vacating office

1. The secretary should complete a form G288 notifying the Registrar of Companies of the director's resignation or other reason for vacating office and this should be submitted to the Registrar within fourteen days of the date of vacation.
2. The company's bankers should be informed and any amendments made to the bank Mandate that are necessary.
3. The secretary should amend the company's Register of Directors and the Register of Directors' Interests.
4. If the director's name is shown on the company's letter heading this should be amended.
5. If the company maintains a Directors' Indemnity Insurance Policy the insurers should be informed.
6. The auditors should be informed.
7. The Inland Revenue should be notified.
8. Any outstanding fees should be paid to the director and arrangements made for the return of any company property – cars, computer equipment, etc.
9. If appropriate, the director should be reminded of any restrictions on his future employment contained in his Contract of Employment with the company.

Notes

If not previously notified, the resignation of a director may be notified on the company's Annual Return shuttle document (form 363S).

Companies House requirements

- Form G288.

References

The Companies Act 1985 S303, S288, S291, S293.
The Company Directors' Disqualification Act 1986.
The Insolvency Act 1986 S14, S103.

Directors – duties

The directors prime responsibility is to manage the company on behalf of and for the benefit of its shareholders as a whole. The extent to which they are authorised to manage the affairs of the company will be set out in the company's Articles of Association. These will normally follow regulation 17 of table A which permits the directors to exercise all powers of the company which are not required to be given by the shareholders of the company either by statute or by the remaining provisions of the Memorandum or Articles of Association.

The directors must ensure that suitable arrangements are in place to enable the company to meet its statutory duties and are liable to penalties if the company is in default. Directors of many companies will delegate these duties to the company secretary and as it is the directors who are liable in the event of default, care must be taken to ensure that the company secretary is suitably qualified.

In many small private companies the directors will rely on their professional advisers. However, directors must act on the advice of their advisers and ensure that the statutory obligations are met. It is the directors and not the professional advisers who are liable and in the event of default and prosecution it is the directors who will be called to account.

Directors' principal statutory responsibility is the preparation of accounts and the report of the directors.

Directors must ensure that the company maintains full and accurate accounting records. The records must be maintained with such accuracy and completeness so that at any time the financial position of the company may be ascertained and so that any balance sheet or profit and loss account gives a true and fair view.

The directors have a duty to prepare a balance sheet and a profit and loss account together with a report to the shareholders in respect of each financial period of the company and to present these accounts to the shareholders and subject to various exemptions to deliver these accounts to the Registrar of Companies.

In addition to the preparation of the accounts the directors prepare a report to be included with the accounts. The report must contain specific information as required by section 235 and schedule 7 of the Companies Act 1985 as follows:

(a) A review of the company's business during the financial year and the position as at the year end.
(b) The amount, if any, of any dividends to be paid.
(c) The names of all the directors who served during the year together with a note of their interests in shares or debentures.
(d) The principal trading activity of the company and any subsidiaries.
(e) Any significant changes in the company's fixed assets.
(f) Any material difference in the value of the assets between the date of the balance sheet and the date of signing of the directors' report.
(g) Any post-balance sheet events likely to have a beneficial or detrimental effect on the company.
(h) If the company employs more than 250 employees the directors' report must contain information on the employment of disabled persons and the particulars of any action taken to encourage participation by the employees in the management of the company.
(i) Details of any shares forfeited or surrendered during the year or shares acquired by a nominee on behalf of the company.
(j) Whether the company has spent more than £200 on political or charitable purposes.

In addition to these accounting duties the directors have a responsibility to disclose their interests in dealings with the company and in particular in respect to the following matters:

Interests in contracts.
Substantial property transactions.
Loans and related dealings.
Compensation for loss of office.
Dealings in options of the shares.
Interests in shares and debentures.

In addition to the above duties and responsibilities criminal and civil liabilities can be imposed on directors who carry on business fraudulently with the intention of defrauding creditors. The directors may have civil liability to make a contribution to the company's assets imposed on them if the company has gone into insolvent liquidation and it can be shown that the directors were aware that the company either was or was about to become insolvent and took no steps to correct the situation or minimise the potential loss to creditors. For these purposes, a director must have displayed the general level of knowledge, skill and experience that might reasonably have been expected of another person carrying out the same role.

As well as the protection offered to shareholders and creditors by the Companies Act 1985, the Company Directors Disqualification Act 1986 provides either for automatic disqualification or allows the courts to make a disqualification order. There are a number of provisions enabling disqualification orders to be made as follows:

1. An undischarged bankrupt may not act as a director or be involved in the formation, promotion or management of a company without the consent of the courts.
2. Where any person fails to make a payment required under an administration order or where Section 492 of the Insolvency Act 1986 applies during a specified period not exceeding two years that person must not without permission of the court act as a director or liquidator or directly or indirectly manage promote or form any company.
3. Courts may disqualify a person from acting as a director or to be involved in the management of a company on the grounds of:
    (a) General misconduct in connection with companies.
    (b) Unfitness.
    (c) Participation in wrongful trading.

References

The Companies Act 1985 S221, S226, S227, S233, S234, S234A, S241, S242, S245, S282–S347 (inclusive). Schedule 7.
The Company Directors' Disqualification Act 1986.

Directors – meetings

There are no fixed rules regarding operation of the Board of Directors. The Articles of Association of the company will stipulate the powers of directors and in these will be stipulated the maximum or minimum number of directors and the quorum necessary for meetings of the directors.

Meetings of the Board of Directors should be held upon 'reasonable' notice, depending upon the particular circumstances of the company or the meeting concerned. Where the Board of Directors all work within the same office, then reasonable notice may well be two to three hours. Where the directors normally only meet on a quarterly basis and do not work at the same location, then reasonable notice may be two weeks.

Meetings are usually called by the secretary on instructions of the chairman, although any director may request the secretary to convene a meeting.

Votes at a directors' meeting are on the basis of one vote per director, although the chairman may be given a casting vote by the Articles of Association.

Directors may be empowered by the Articles of Association of the company to appoint an alternate to attend and vote in their place, when circumstances dictate that they are unable to attend the meeting themselves.

In addition to the use of Written Resolutions, the Articles of Association of the company may contain provisions allowing directors' meetings to be held by conference telephone or conference video equipment so that meetings may be held whilst the directors remain in different offices or indeed in different countries.

Although the day-to-day running of the company will be left to the managing director and the other executive directors, the Board should meet to decide upon matters of policy and matters requiring signature on behalf of the Board. Such matters would include the following:

allotment and transfer of shares, opening of bank accounts and changing of bank Mandates, convening of shareholders' meetings, declaration of dividends, changes of auditors, solicitors or other professional advisers, any matter requiring execution under the company seal or, where the company does not have a seal, executed on behalf of the company, etc.

Minutes of the decisions of the Board of Directors should be kept and made available to directors for inspection if they so wish.

Shareholders have no authority to view the minutes of the directors.

References

The Companies Act 1985 S382, S382A.

Directors – removal

Irrespective of any provisions contained in the company's Articles of Association, the shareholders can, at any time, remove a director by Ordinary Resolution.

Procedure

1. A company must be given Special Notice of the shareholders' intention to propose as an Ordinary Resolution a resolution to remove the particular director.
2. Upon receipt of the notice the company must forward a copy to the director concerned.
3. At a meeting of the directors the directors should convene an Extraordinary General Meeting to consider the resolution.
4. The Secretary issues to the shareholders a notice convening the Extraordinary General Meeting. The notice must state on it that Special Notice has been given.
5. The Extraordinary General Meeting should be held.

Notes

The director to be removed has the right to circulate to the shareholders of the company a statement setting out details of why he should not be removed; he also has the right to be heard at the Extraordinary General Meeting.

Although the meeting can be held at short notice without contravening the provisions relating to the giving of Special Notice, this may be seen as prejudicial to the director's case and care must be taken when convening the meeting upon short notice.

Although the shareholders can remove the director from office, this would not prejudice the directors' rights under any service contract, nor would it affect his ability to take action against the company for any breach. The procedure for directors ceasing to hold office (see page 39) should also be considered and followed where appropriate.

Companies House requirements

- Form G288.

Notes

The removal of a director must be put to a meeting of the members and cannot be dealt with by way of a written resolution.

References

The Companies Act 1985 S303, S304, S379.

Dissolution

The Registrar of Companies has authority under certain circumstances to dissolve a company and to remove it from the Register if it is believed to be no longer trading and redundant. This authority is contained in Section 652 of the Companies Act 1985.

The power can be exercised directly by the Registrar or at the request of the directors of the company concerned.

Procedure

1. Ensure that all liabilities have been satisfied or waived.
2. Obtain Inland Revenue clearance (by way of an extra statutory concession) to enable any distribution of assets to be treated as a capital distribution and not a revenue distribution (Income and Corporation Taxes Act 1988 Section 209(1)).
3. Ensure that all assets are transferred to the shareholders as a distribution in specie including title to leases, property, investments, etc.
4. The company's bank account should be closed and any funds remaining distributed to the shareholders.
5. Ensure that all outstanding Inland Revenue assessments have been vacated.
6. Write to the Registrar requesting dissolution of the company.
7. The Registrar will require that a director makes a declaration to the effect that the company is not trading and not required, and will supply a form of certificate for signature and return.
8. The Registrar will publish a notice in the *London Gazette* that the company is to be dissolved in three months' time unless any objections are received.
9. Where an objection has been received, the Registrar will inform the company that there has been such an objection. The most common

50 COMPANY SECRETARIAL CHECKLISTS

objections are from the Inland Revenue in instances where Corporation Tax Assessments are outstanding. In these circumstances it is necessary to clear these outstanding assessments with the Revenue and then make a further request to the Registrar for the company to be dissolved.
10. If there are no objections raised on the publication of the notice, at the expiration of the three-month period the Registrar will formally dissolve the company and remove its name from the Register.

Notes

If the directors knowingly allow a company to be dissolved which has liabilities, these liabilities pass to the directors personally.

Any assets remaining in the company's name will pass to the Crown and any bank accounts maintained by the company will be frozen.

In such circumstances it will be necessary to have the company restored to the Register (see page 114).

It is important not to file any forms, annual returns or accounts with the Registrar once dissolution has been requested as the Registrar will assume that the company is now required and will take no further action.

References

The Companies Act 1985 S652.
The Income and Corporation Taxes Act 1988 S209.

Dividends

Unless shares of any particular class carry a fixed dividend, the declaration and payment of a dividend is at the directors' discretion.

The dividends can only be paid if the company has sufficient distributable profits.

The directors may declare a dividend as they see fit in the case of an interim dividend, or subject to the approval of the shareholders in general meeting in the case of the final dividend.

The declaration on an interim dividend should be made by reference to the management accounts and does not require consent of the shareholders in general meeting.

The payment of a final dividend will be made by reference to the audited accounts and, in the circumstances where the audited accounts have a qualified Audit Report, it will be necessary for the auditors to report to the shareholders that the matter of their qualification is not material for the purposes of declaring a dividend. Any payment of the final dividend is subject to confirmation by the shareholders who may decrease the size of the dividend but have no power to increase it.

Procedure

Interim dividend

1. The Board of Directors approve the declaration of an interim dividend.
2. The secretary arranges the printing of dividend warrants and tax vouchers.
3. Dividend warrants and tax vouchers are despatched to the shareholders.

52 COMPANY SECRETARIAL CHECKLISTS

Final dividend

4. Directors recommend a final dividend.
5. Accounts and notice of general meeting are issued to shareholders. If accounts have a qualified Audit Report, the auditors' statement on their qualification is circulated with the accounts.
6. The general meeting is held.
7. If approval is given to the final dividend, the secretary arranges payment as in 2 and 3 above.

Notes

The secretary should liaise with the bank concerning the format of the dividend warrant.

Schedule of payments and non-cashed cheques must be maintained. Often companies maintain a separate dividend account.

References

The Companies Act 1985 S263, S270, S271.

Documents – retention periods

Type of document	Period of retention
Certificate of Incorporation	Original should be kept permanently
Certificate to Commence Business (public company)	Original to be kept permanently
Board minutes	Originals to be kept permanently
Minutes of general and class meetings	Originals to be kept permanently
Annual Report and Accounts	Signed copy to be kept permanently (A stock of spare copies should be maintained for up to five years to meet casual requests)
Trust Deeds	Originals to be kept permanently
Circulars to shareholders including notices of meetings	Master copy to be kept permanently
Memorandum and Articles of Association	Original copy to be kept permanently
Seal Book/Register	Original to be kept permanently
Proxy forms/Polling cards	One month if no poll demanded; one year if poll demanded
Register of Directors and Secretaries, Register of Directors' Interests, Register of Interests in Voting Shares, Register of Charges, Register of Members	Originals to be kept permanently
Register of Debenture or Loan Stock Holders	Seven years after redemption of stock

54 COMPANY SECRETARIAL CHECKLISTS

Forms for application of shares, debentures, etc., forms of acceptance and transfer, Renounceable Letters of Acceptance and Allotment, Renounceable Share Certificates	Originals to be kept permanently
Request for designation or redesignation of accounts, letters of request, allotment sheets	Originals to be kept permanently
Letters of Indemnity for lost Share Certificates	All originals to be kept permanently
Stop Notices and other Court Orders	Originals to be kept permanently
Powers of Attorney	Copies to be retained permanently
Dividend and interest bank Mandate forms	Original to be kept until account closed
Cancelled Share or Stock Certificates	One year
Notification of change of address	Two years
Any contract or memorandum to purchase the company's own shares	Ten years
Report of an interest in voting shares for investigations requisitioned by members	Six years
Register of Interest in Shares when company ceases to be a public company	Six years
Contracts with customers, suppliers or agents	Six years after expiry
Licensing agreements	Six years after expiry
Rental and hire purchase agreements	Six years after expiry
Indemnities and guarantees	Six years after expiry
Deeds of Title	Permanently
Leases	Twelve years after lease has terminated
Agreements with architects, builders, etc.	Six years after contract completion
Patent and trade mark records	Permanently
Accounting records required by the Companies Acts	Six years for a public company; three years for a private company
Taxation Returns and records	Permanently

DOCUMENTS – RETENTION PERIODS 55

Internal Financial Reports	Five years
Statements and instructions to banks	Six years
Staff personnel records	Seven years after employment ceases
Patent agreements with staff	Twenty years after employment ceases
Applications for jobs	Up to twelve months
Payroll records	Twelve years
Salary registers	Five years
Tax Returns	Permanently
Expense accounts	Seven years
Employment agreements	Permanently
Time cards and piece-work records	Two years
Wages records	Five years
Medical records	Twelve years
Industrial training records	Six years
Accident books	Twelve years
Trustees and rules (pension schemes)	Permanently
Trustees' Minute Book	Permanently
Pension fund annual accounts and Inland Revenue approvals	Permanently
Investment records	Permanently
Actuarial valuation records	Permanently
Contribution records	Permanently
Records of ex-pensioners	Six years after cessation of benefit
Pension scheme investment policies	Twelve years after cessation
Group health policies	Twelve years after final cessation of benefit
Group personal accident policies	Twelve years after cessation of benefit
Public liability policies	Permanently
Product liability policies	Permanently
Employers' liability policies	Permanently
Sundry insurance policies	Three years after lapse
Claims correspondence	Three years after settlement
Accident reports and relevant correspondence	Three years after settlement
Insurance schedules	Ten years
Customs and Excise Returns	Five years

56 COMPANY SECRETARIAL CHECKLISTS

Vehicle registration records, MOT Certificates and vehicle maintenance records	Two years after disposal of vehicle
Certificates and other documents of Title	Permanently or until investment disposed of

Dormant companies

To qualify as a dormant company, the company must fulfil one of the following criteria:

1. The company must remain dormant from the time of its incorporation and exempt itself from the obligation to appoint auditors before the first AGM; or
2. The company must have been dormant since the end of the previous financial year, qualify as a small company or would be eligible if not part of an ineligible group and be exempt from preparing group accounts. Such a company may resolve not to appoint auditors at any general meeting or a meeting called to consider the accounts.

'Dormant' means that no significant accounting transactions have arisen during the financial period.

Dormant companies are still required to file non-trading accounts and an Annual Return with the Registrar of Companies. All expenses incurred by the company, in particular the Annual Return filing fee must be paid either by the directors or by the shareholders or by a holding company directly.

Once a dormant company commences to trade or has any income, for instance bank interest, the company ceases to be dormant. There is no particular filing requirement necessary when a company recommences trading. The company must, however, appoint auditors and prepare audited accounts for the financial period.

Notes

See Accounts – dormant companies (page 5)

58 COMPANY SECRETARIAL CHECKLISTS

Companies House requirements

- Special resolution not to appoint auditors.

References

The Companies Act 1985 S250, S246, S221.

Elective Resolutions

This form of resolution enables private companies to opt out of certain obligations. Elective Resolutions are only available to private companies. The following concessions can be gained:

> Directors may be authorised to allot shares pursuant to Section 80 of the Companies Act 1985 for an indefinite period in excess of five years.
> The company may dispense with the laying of accounts before its members.
> The company may dispense with the requirement to hold an Annual General Meeting.
> The company may dispense with the annual appointment of auditors.
> The company may reduce the majority required for short notice from 95 per cent of the members entitled to attend and vote to 90 per cent.

Procedure to approve Elective Resolutions

1. Elective Resolutions require the approval of all the members entitled to attend and vote at a General Meeting. If the resolution is passed by Resolution in Writing, it will require unanimity from the shareholders.
2. The meeting must be convened upon twenty-one clear days' notice.
3. The notice must state that the resolutions are to be passed as Elective Resolutions and state the terms of the resolutions.
4. Elective Resolutions require unanimity of those entitled to attend and vote and not just those present.
5. An Elective Resolution may be revoked at any time by Ordinary Resolution.

60 COMPANY SECRETARIAL CHECKLISTS

6. Where a private company is re-registered as a public company, any Elective Resolutions in force immediately cease to have effect.
7. A copy of the Elective Resolutions should be filed with the Registrar of Companies within fifteen days.
8. Any resolution revoking an Elective Resolution must be filed with the Registrar within fifteen days.

Notes

Although not required to hold an Annual General Meeting, the company must still issue to its members a copy of the audited accounts. In addition, the accounts must be accompanied by a notice saying that there will not be an Annual General Meeting unless, not less than twenty-eight days before the time for filing the accounts with the Registrar expires, a request to convene the meeting has been received from a member or the auditor. Notwithstanding that an Annual General Meeting has been requested and held, the Elective regime remains in force.

Companies House requirements

- Copy of Elective resolution.

References

The Companies Act 1985 S80A, S366A, S369A, S378, S379A.

Extraordinary General Meetings

Any meeting which is not an Annual General Meeting is an Extraordinary General Meeting.

The procedure to convene an Extraordinary General Meeting is as follows:

1. The Board of Directors should meet and resolve to convene an Extraordinary General Meeting and authorise the secretary to issue a notice convening the meeting, stipulating the date and place of the meeting.
2. A notice should be issued to the members allowing fourteen days' clear notice where the meeting is to consider an Ordinary Resolution, and twenty-one days' clear notice where the meeting is to consider a Special or Extraordinary Resolution.
3. The meeting may be held upon shorter notice if 95 per cent of the members entitled to attend and vote agree. This level of 95 per cent agreement may be reduced to 90 per cent by Elective Resolution.
4. Copies of the resolutions, if approved, should be filed with the Registrar of Companies within fifteen days.

Companies House requirements

- Copies of approved resolutions, where appropriate (see page 106).

References

The Companies Act 1985 S369, S370, S378.

Extraordinary General Meetings – requisition

A member or members holding not less than 10 per cent of the paid-up issued share capital and carrying the right to vote may requisition a meeting of the members.

Procedure

1. A Letter of Requisition and the text of the desired resolution must be received at the company's Registered Office.
2. The directors must convene the meeting within twenty-one days of receipt.
3. If the directors do not convene a meeting within twenty-one days, the requisitionists may convene the meeting themselves for a date not more than three months thereafter.
4. The directors are deemed not to have duly convened the meeting if convened for a date more than twenty-eight days after the date of the notice.

Notes

The secretary should ensure that the requisitions do hold at least 10 per cent of the voting shares.

Once the notice has been issued by either the company or the requisitionists, the procedure for holding the meeting is the same as for an Extraordinary General Meeting.

If the resolution is for the removal of a director or the auditor, the special notice procedure must be followed (see pages 22 and 47).

References

The Companies Act 1985 S368.

Forfeiture

When shares have been allotted as either nil or partly paid, the balance outstanding on the shares can be called at any time by the directors (see page 34). The amount of a call can be all or part of the balance outstanding.

Any shares on which a call has been made and which remains outstanding may be forfeited.

It is necessary for the procedures for making a call and subsequent forfeiture to be strictly adhered to; otherwise, any forfeiture may be overturned by the courts.

Procedure

1. It will be necessary to examine the company's Articles of Association for the exact procedure to be followed. In most circumstances, however, the procedure for forfeiture will follow that laid down by Table A.
2. If a call remains unpaid, the directors shall give to the member not less than fourteen days' notice requiring payment of all outstanding amounts and must state that if the notice is not complied with, the shares are liable to forfeiture.
3. If the call remains unpaid, then the shares may be forfeited by resolution of the directors.
4. Notice of Forfeiture is usually sent to the shareholder but it is not a requirement.
5. Forfeited shares may be sold or cancelled as the directors see fit.
6. If the shareholder can not or will not pay the call, he may wish to surrender the shares. The shares can only be surrendered if they are already liable to be forfeited.
7. Details of the forfeiture must be entered in the Register of Members.

Notes

The member whose shares have been forfeited ceases to be a member in respect of such shares as soon as the forfeiture has been entered in the Register of Members. Such person does, however, remain liable for any amounts unpaid on the shares.

Forfeited shares may be sold or disposed of on such terms and in such manner as the directors think fit. Forfeited shares that are re-issued must be issued at a price not less than the amounts remaining unpaid. When shares are re-issued, the original member will no longer be liable for the uncalled amounts once the full amount has been received by the company, from whatever source.

Where the shares are re-issued at a price greater than the unpaid amount then the company shall pay to the original member the additional monies received up to the amount paid by them.

At the end of the financial year it will be necessary to inform the auditors that certain shares have been forfeited and whether or not they have been re-issued.

Headed paper

The following information must be shown on all company business letters and certain other documentation as listed:

> The full name of the company as registered must be shown on all letters, notices and other official publications, bills of exchange, promissory notes, cheques and orders for money or goods signed by or on behalf of the company, invoices, receipts and letters of credit. If this provision is not complied with, the signatory of the document in question may be personally liable in the event of default by the company.
>
> Where the company operates under a trading name other than its registered name, the registered name will usually be shown at the foot of the page.
>
> The place of registration must be shown, i.e. registered in England and Wales, Cardiff, Wales, Scotland or Edinburgh.
>
> The company's registration number.
>
> The address of the company's Registered Office. Where the company's business address and Registered Office are the same, the fact that the address shown on the headed paper is the Registered Office must be stated.
>
> When a company changes its Registered Office, the company's headed paper must be changed to show the new address within fourteen days of the date of change. The date of change is the date of receipt of the form G287 by the Registrar of Companies.
>
> Where the company is an investment company, this fact must be stated on the headed paper.
>
> In the case of a charity where the company's name does not include the word 'Charity' or 'Charitable', the fact that it is a charity must be stated on the headed paper. If this provision is not complied with, the signatory to any documents may be personally liable in the event of default.

Where directors' names are shown on headed paper, all the directors' names must be shown and not just some of them. This is particularly important to remember where the directors have personalised stationery.
It is no longer necessary to show the nationality of directors.

References

The Companies Act 1985 S287, S349, S351.

Incorporation

The majority of companies are formed on behalf of the ultimate owners by registration agents. It is open to anyone, however, to incorporate a company by the following procedure:

Procedure

1. Check the index of company names maintained by the Registrar of Companies to ensure that the proposed name is not the same as or too similar to the name of an existing company.
2. Additionally, certain words –'sensitive' words – may require justification or approval by some third party. A list of sensitive words is shown on page 122.
3. The following documents must be submitted to the Registrar of Companies:
   (i) The Memorandum of Association. This must be signed by the subscriber(s) in the presence of at least one witness.
   (ii) Following the implementation of the Companies (single member private companies) regulations 1992 it is no longer necessary for private companies to have two or more shareholders. Public companies still require at least two shareholders.
   (iii) Articles of Association which again must be signed by the subscriber(s) and the signature(s) witnessed.
   (iv) A statement containing the names and addresses of the first director(s), secretary and the situation of the Registered Office on form G10. This form must be signed by the first directors and secretary, agreeing to act in that capacity, and must also be signed by the subscriber(s) or agents.
   (v) A statutory declaration on form G12 made by a solicitor or by one of the first directors or secretary confirming that the

necessary documents have been properly prepared. This declaration must be sworn before a solicitor.
(vi) Where appropriate, formal justification of the name must be submitted with the incorporation papers.
(vii) The registration fee payable (currently £50; same-day fee £200).

Notes

Upon incorporation the Registrar of Companies issues a Certificate of Incorporation which shows the date of incorporation, states the status of the company (i.e. private or public) and shows the company's registered number.

A private company is entitled to commence business immediately and there is no requirement for the company to obtain a certificate to commence business.

The incorporation process for a public company is essentially the same as for a private company with the exception that the form of Memorandum and Articles of Association is different and that the company must have a minimum authorised share capital of £50,000.

A public company must be incorporated with at least two subscribers, each holding at least one share.

Before a public company may commence business, it must apply for a certificate to commence business and to borrow. This certificate will only be issued once the company has a nominal issued capital of at least £50,000 with each share at least 25 per cent paid up.

Companies House requirements

- Forms G10, G12.
- Copy of memorandum and Articles of Association (signed).
- Registration fee.
- Justification of name if necessary.

References

The Companies Act 1985 S1, S2, S3, S7, S8, S10, S11, S13, S117.
The Companies (single member private companies) regulations 1992.

Incorporation – first board meeting

Once a company has been incorporated there are a number of matters that should be formally noted or approved by the directors.

1. The first directors, secretary and situation of the Registered Office will have been determined and shown on the form G10 filed with the Registrar of Companies. Particularly where companies are incorporated by registration agents, the first director and secretary will resign and the Registered Office will be changed immediately following incorporation. Any changes should be formally approved by the Board and forms G288 and G287 filed with the Registrar.
2. If the company is to adopt a company seal, this should be formally approved by the directors. It is no longer necessary for a company to have a seal, as the company may rely on Section 36A of the Companies Act 1985. If the company does rely on this Section, documents executed by the directors must be expressed as having been executed on behalf of the company ie 'Executed as a deed this ... day of ... 1992 on behalf of ... Limited in the presence of ....'

The directors at this time may also wish to consider some of the following matters:

1. Appoint a managing director or chairman of the Board.
2. Appoint bankers, including approval of the relevant bank Mandate.
3. Appoint solicitors to act on behalf of the company.
4. Appoint accountants and auditors.
5. Set the company's accounting reference date.
6. Approve the transfer of the subscriber shares, if appropriate.
7. Allot shares in the capital of the company and approve the issue of Share Certificates.
8. Dispense with the need for distinguishing numbers on fully paid shares.

9. Notify the Registrar, if appropriate, of the place where directors' service contracts and the statutory books are situated, if other than at the Registered Office.
10. Some or all of the directors may require service contracts.
11. The directors may decide to effect directors' indemnity insurance.

Consider arrangements regarding PAYE, VAT, insurance and the possible need to register trade marks in the company's name.

The appropriate company headed stationery should be obtained. This should contain the company's full name, Registered Office, the place of registration (i.e. England and Wales or Scotland) and the company's registration number. Although it is permissible to have the directors' names shown on the headed paper, these must either *all* be given or not at all (see page 66).

A form G224 notifying the Registrar of the company's accounting reference date should be submitted to the Registrar within nine months of incorporation. If a form is not received by the Registrar within this time, the company will be deemed to have as its accounting reference date the last day of the month of the anniversary of its incorporation. If a company subsequently decides to have a different accounting reference date, it will be necessary to amend the accounting reference date deemed to have been given to the company, on form G225(1) (see page 1).

Companies House requirements

- G288, G287, G88(2), G224, as required.

References

The Companies Act 1985 S10, S88, S224, S287, S288.

Joint shareholders

Occasionally, shares will be issued to two or more persons. The Articles of Association of the company may place a limit on the number of holders. Under stock exchange rules, quoted public companies must allow for a minimum of four joint holders.

Listed below are suggested solutions to particular problems or queries than can arise, in relation to joint holdings.

Joint holders may request that the shares registered in their names be split into two or more accounts with the holders' names being shown in a different order. Such requests are commonly dealt with without the need for a stock transfer form, provided the request is in writing and signed by all the joint holders. Additionally, it will be necessary for the Share Certificate to be returned for cancellation and the issue of new certificates. For ease of administration, however, companies may prefer to deal with such requests by designation of accounts rather than by re-arranging the order of the names.

Occasionally, the joint holders will request that the order of the names on the joint account be changed and again most companies will process this without the need for a formal stock transfer form, provided the request is in writing, signed by all the joint holders and includes confirmation that no sale or disposition has taken place. Again, the Share Certificate should be returned for cancellation. All communications for the shareholders will be sent to the first-named of the joint holders.

The joint holders may request that communications be sent to someone other than the first-named; however, for administrative reasons this may be impractical for the company. Additionally, the Articles of Association may prohibit such a request.

Joint shareholders – death of one shareholder

When a joint shareholder dies, the surviving holder or holders in whose name or names the shares are registered become the sole beneficiaries of the share.

The company will require sight of the Death Certificate or an authenticated copy of it. The Register of Members should be amended to note the death of one holder.

The company may require a new dividend mandate to be given.

The Share Certificate may be either endorsed or cancelled and a new certificate issued.

Loan stock

The procedure for the issue of loan stock and thereafter the payment of any interest and the holding of meetings are, subject to the trust deed creating the loan stock, similar to the procedures for the issue, declaration of dividend and requirements for meetings of ordinary shares.

The most important difference is that the loan stock will be created by a trust deed setting out the rights attaching to the stock.

The trust deed should cover the following points:

1. Details of the stock, aggregate amount of stock, the units in which it may be issued or transferred and details of repayment and interest.
2. Provisions creating a charge over the company's assets and stipulating under what circumstances the security is enforceable.
3. The powers of the trustee. In particular the trustee is usually instructed to concur with the company in all dealings relating to the charged assets.
4. Provisions stipulating that no additional charges can be created ranking ahead of the stock without written consent of the loan stockholders.
5. Schedules detailing the repayment conditions, transfer conditions, regulations for meetings and the form of stock certificate.

Notes

The company is not required by statute to keep a register of stock holders. However, for practical reasons this is usually done and in such circumstances the register of loan stock holders should be in the same form as the register of members.

LOAN STOCK

Stock is issued by resolution of the directors as with the share capital although there is no requirement to file a return with the Registrar of Companies.

Companies House requirements

- Copy of trust deed charging the company's assets.

Loan stock – convertable

It is common for the terms of issue of loan stock (more usually *unsecured* loan stock) to include provisions for the loan stock to be converted into share capital. Usually the loan stock will be convertable into Equity Shares, although the stock may be convertable into another class of shares. When conversion of the stock is due, the following procedure should be maintained:

1. Where conversion is at the option of the company or stock is convertible over a number of months or years, the directors should authorise the conversion of the stock, whether in full or in part. The precise procedures to be followed will be stipulated in the Loan Stock Deed.
2. The secretary should prepare a circular letter to the holders giving details of the conversion procedure, including a Form of Nomination and Acceptance for their use. A Form of Nomination is necessary in the event that any particular stockholder requires the shares to be registered in another person's name.
3. As the completed Notices of Conversion and Forms of Nomination and Acceptance are received, these should be checked against the Register of Stockholders to ensure that the details are correct. The loan stock certificates should be returned for cancellation. Once the period for conversion has elapsed, a list of shares to be issued should be compiled and the directors should formally allot the shares. A Return of Allotments should be submitted to the Registrar of Companies within fifteen days.
4. Share Certificates evidencing the shares issued should be prepared and issued to the shareholders within two months of the date of allotment.
5. The Register of Members should be amended to record the shares

now issued and the Register of Loan Stock should be amended to show the loan stock that has been cancelled.
6. Where the conversion of the loan stock is only for part of the stock, a balancing loan stock certificate should be issued.

Companies House requirements

- G88(2), G88(3).

References

The Companies Act 1985 S80, S88.

Loan stock – unsecured

Unsecured loan stock carries a greater risk for investors than secured loan stock and as a result will usually attract a higher rate of interest. Additionally, as an added incentive, the holders may be given options to acquire equity capital in the future, usually by conversion of the unsecured loan stock into Equity Shares rather than by repayment of the loan. As with secured loan stock, the issue of unsecured loan stock and the rights and privileges attaching to the stock are governed by a Trust Deed covering the following points:

1. Details of the terms of issue, amounts payable on the stock and, where these are payable by more than one instalment, dates and terms of the instalments, details of the repayment or redemption of the stock and interest payments, and any rights of conversion or options on shares in the capital of the company.
2. Restrictions on further issues of unsecured loanstock without the approval of the existing loan stockholders.
3. Restriction on the borrowing powers of the company without prior approval.
4. Restrictions on the disposal by the company of certain assets or other sale agreements without prior approval.
5. Guarantees by the company that it will maintain sufficient unissued share capital to satisfy any conversion or option rights given to the loan stockholders.
6. The actions open to the stockholders in the event of non-payment of interest or non-redemption of the stock on the due date.
7. Details of the trustees to the issue and of any remuneration payable.
8. Schedules containing the form of stock certificate, option certificates, notices of redemption and detailed conditions concerning the redemption, whether in whole or in part, and any conversion rights or options given to the holders.

LOAN STOCK – UNSECURED

The procedures to be followed for the issue or repayment of unsecured loan stock are the same as for loan stock (see page 74).

The conversion procedure, where relevant, is the same as for convertible loan stock (see page 76).

Memorandum of Association

The Memorandum of Association of a company sets out the following details:

  Company name
  Place of incorporation
  Company's objects
  The liability of the members
  The authorised share capital

The company's name and its objects can be altered by Special Resolution of the members (see page 81).

The authorised share capital can be increased by Ordinary Resolution (see page 26).

It is possible to alter the liability of the members from limited to unlimited or vice versa by re-registration of the company (see pages 95–102).

In any of the above cases a copy of the amending resolution, together with an amended copy of the Memorandum of Association, must be filed with the Registrar of Companies within fifteen days of its approval.

Variation of the share capital will often require a consequential alteration of the Articles by Special Resolution (see page 15).

When the share capital has been altered, the Memorandum of Association should contain details of all changes to the share capital of the company from its incorporation. A similar history should be shown where the company has changed its name.

References

The Companies Act 1985 S2–S6, S18.

Name change

A company may change its name by Special Resolution of the members.

Certain words are deemed to be 'sensitive' and require justification or due authority before the Registrar of Companies will allow their use. A list of sensitive words and the authority required for their use is shown on page 122.

Procedure

1. Check availability of name.
2. Check that no trade marks are infringed.
3. Check that name does not contain a sensitive word – if it does, justification will be required.
4. The directors should convene a Board meeting to convene a meeting of the shareholders.
5. Notice of the meeting must be issued to the members upon twenty-one clear days' notice unless Agreement to Short Notice is given by the members.
6. Once the Extraordinary General Meeting has been held and the resolution passed, a copy of the resolution must be submitted to the Registrar within fifteen days, together with the change-of-name fee payable (currently £50; same-day fee £200).
7. Once the Registrar has issued the Certificate of Incorporation on Change of Name, it will be necessary to obtain new headed stationery, and a new company seal where the company has a seal.
8. Arrange for the name of the company's bank accounts to be changed and arrange for the company's Memorandum and Articles of Association to be amended and reprinted.
9. Notify the company's suppliers and customers of the change of name (ie British Telecom), the VAT authorities, Inland Revenue, etc. Signs

81

at the company's premises or on the company's cars, vans and lorries will also require amendment.

Companies House requirements

- Copy of Special Resolution
- Registration fee.
- Justification, as appropriate.

References

The Companies Act 1985 S26, S28, S29, S30, S31.
The Companies and Business Names Regulations 1981.

Notices

The notice periods for meetings are as follows:

1. Annual General Meeting — 21 days
2. Extraordinary General Meeting
   - (a) Special Resolutions — 21 days
   - (b) Elective Resolutions — 21 days
   - (c) Ordinary Resolutions — 14 days
   - (d) Extraordinary Resolutions — 14 days
   - (e) Ordinary Resolutions of an unlimited company — 7 days
3. Resolutions requiring Special Notice
   - (a) Notice to company of intention to put resolution — 28 days
   - (b) Notice to members — 21 days

Notices convening meetings to consider Special, Extraordinary or Elective Resolutions must state that the resolutions are to be put as Special, Extraordinary or Elective, as appropriate.

Notes

Period of notice is stated in 'clear' days. The Articles should be consulted to ascertain what constitutes 'clear' days for the particular company. For example the company's Articles may state that the day of receipt must be classed as forty-eight hours and not twenty-four hours after posting (see also page 10).

References

The Companies Act 1985 S369.

Pre-emption rights – allotment

Section 89(1) of the Companies Act 1985 provides that any new shares to be issued by a company must first be offered pro rata to the existing shareholders. This provision safeguards shareholders as their holding of shares can only be diluted if they do not take up shares. However, private companies may forgo these provisions in their Articles of Association and either substitute 'tailor made' pre-emption provisions or delete pre-emption provisions entirely. Public companies may only relax these provisions by special resolution. Many private companies are incorporated with Articles of Association that remove the provisions of Section 89(1) and substitute alternative provisions. Commonly the first allotment following incorporation is exempt from any pre-emption provisions.

The following procedure should be followed by private companies wishing to issue new shares where there are pre-emption provisions:

Procedure

1. Check the company's Articles of Association to establish what the exact pre-emption provisions are.
2. If the company has only a small number of shareholders it may be practical to arrange for the shareholders to waive their pre-emption rights by notice in writing.
3. For companies with a large number of shareholders this may not be possible and accordingly the rights should be waived by special resolution at an EGM. For procedure see page 61.
4. This waiver of pre-emption rights is usually limited to a specific issue of shares and not a blanket waiver.

Notes

It is not necessary to waive pre-emption rights for a rights, bonus or capitalisation issue as these are pro-rata issues.

Where there is more than one class of shares, each class may have different pre-emption rights.

Public companies usually authorise the directors to issue up to 5% new shares without pre-emption rights applying, annually at each AGM, such authority lapsing at the next AGM.

Companies House requirements

- A copy of the special resolution as appropriate.

References

The Companies Act 1985 S89–S96 (inclusive).

Pre-emption rights – transfer

There are no statutory pre-emption rights on the transfer of shares. However, many private companies and some public companies will have pre-emption rights embodied within their Articles of Association. Although the provisions usually stipulate a strict procedure to follow when shares are to be transferred, these provisions are frequently waived in the circumstances where the transfer is agreed by all the shareholders. The provisions would, however, be used in a contentious transfer. In such circumstances the pre-emption provisions must be followed strictly.

Procedure

1. Check Articles of Association to see whether pre-emption rights apply to the transfer.
2. If the share transfer is not contentious it may be appropriate for the existing shareholders to waive their rights of pre-emption by notice in writing.
3. Alternatively the transfer may be non-contentious but due to the large number of shareholders the rights of pre-emption may best be waived by special resolution at an EGM. For procedure see page 61.
4. Where the transfer is likely to be contentious or it is deemed inappropriate for the shareholders to waive their rights of pre-emption it will be necessary strictly to follow the pre-emption procedure as set down in the Articles. These procedures will often take a number of weeks to complete and may require the company's auditors to certify a fair value for the shares.

Notes

Where a company's Articles of Association do contain pre-emption rights on transfer there may be special dispensations for transfers between family members or group companies.

Where shares are to be transferred following the death of a shareholder the pre-emption provisions may be deemed to have been brought into effect and the shares offered to the existing shareholders even if the appropriate notice has not been given by the executor(s).

Companies House requirements

- A copy of the special resolution waiving the pre-emption rights as appropriate.

Purchase of own shares

It is possible under certain circumstances for a company to purchase its own shares (other than shares issued as redeemable on issue) provided that the purchase is authorised by the company's Articles of Association. Additionally, there are restrictions on the company's ability to use its reserves to purchase its own shares and care must be taken to ensure that the company has sufficient distributable reserves for the purpose. It may also be possible for the company to issue new shares to fund the redemption or, in the case of private companies, to redeem shares out of capital (see page 92).

Procedure

1. The terms of the agreement by which the company is to acquire its own shares must be approved by special resolution of the members. Alternatively, the purchase may be authorised under a contingent purchase contract which has previously been authorised by the shareholders by Special Resolution. Such authority may be varied or revoked or renewed by Special Resolution.
2. In the case of a public company the resolution must state the date upon which the authority is to lapse, being not more than eighteen months from the date of the resolution.
3. A copy of the agreement, or a written schedule of its terms if the contract is not in writing, must be made available for inspection by the members of the company at the company's Registered Office for not less than fifteen days prior to the meeting and at the meeting itself. The schedule of the terms must include the names of any members holding shares which it is proposed be purchased and, if the written contract does not show these names, a schedule must be attached showing the names and the number of shares to which the

contract relates. Where a previously approved contract is being varied, the terms of the variation must be available for inspection by the members.
4. This requirement for the documents to be made available for inspection to the members prior to the meeting restricts the ability of the company to hold the meeting at shorter notice than fifteen days. Where the resolutions are to be passed by Written Resolution of the members, a copy of the contract and/or any schedule must be supplied to the members no later than the date upon which they receive a copy of the Written Resolution for signature.
5. The resolution will be invalid if any member of the company holding shares which it is proposed be re-purchased exercises the voting rights attaching to those shares, and the resolution would not have been passed if those shares had not been voted.
6. Copies of the Special Resolution must be submitted to the Registrar of Companies within fifteen days of its approval.
7. Once the company has purchased the shares, a Return on form G169 must be submitted to the Registrar, stating the number of shares and the class of shares together with the nominal value of the shares and the date on which they were re-purchased. The re-purchase of shares by a company is subject to stamp duty, the duty being payable on the consideration and not the nominal value.

Companies House requirements

- Copy of Special Resolution.
- Form G169.

References

The Companies Act 1985 S159–S170 (inclusive).

Purchase of own shares – financial assistance

As a general rule the Companies Acts prohibits the giving of financial assistance by a company, whether directly or indirectly, for the purpose of acquiring its own shares or those of its holding company, before or after the event.

There are, however, a number of exemptions which are set out in S153–S155 of the Companies Act 1985. For most purposes these are only available to private companies.

Procedure

1. The directors must make a Statutory Declaration on form G155(6)(a) or (b), containing details of the assistance to be given and details of the person to whom the assistance is to be given. Where the assistance is to be given for the purposes of acquiring shares in its holding company, a similar declaration must be given by the directors of that holding company and of any other subsidiary that is also a subsidiary of that holding company.
2. The declaration must also state that in the directors' opinion, once the assistance has been given, the company will be able to meet its debts as they become due.
3. Attached to the Statutory Declaration should be a report by the company's auditors stating that they have made enquiries into the state of affairs of the company and that there is nothing stated in the directors' declaration that is unreasonable in the circumstances.
4. The giving of financial assistance must be approved by resolution of the shareholders of the company giving the financial assistance and a copy of the Statutory Declaration and the Auditors' Report must be available for inspection at the meeting.
5. If it is proposed that approval by the members is to be given by

Written Resolution, a copy of the Statutory Declaration and a copy of the Auditors' Report must be supplied to each member at or before the time they are supplied with the Written Resolution for signature.
6. If the proposed financial assistance is to be given for the acquisition of shares in the company's holding company, it is necessary for the shareholders of the holding company also to approve the financial assistance by Special Resolution and, if the companies involved are in a group structure and there are intermediate holding companies between the company giving the financial assistance and the company whose shares are to be acquired, these intermediate holding companies must also approve the giving of the financial assistance, unless they are *wholly owned* subsidiaries.
7. The Special Resolutions must be approved within one week of the date of the Statutory Declaration made by the directors.
8. The Statutory Declaration and the Auditors' Report must be delivered to the Registrar of Companies together with copies of the Special Resolutions or Written Resolutions within fifteen days of the passing of the resolutions.
9. Once approval has been given, the financial assistance may not be given until four weeks have elapsed from the date of approval, unless all the shareholders entitled to attend and vote at the meeting voted in favour of the resolution. Additionally, the assistance must have been given within eight weeks of approval of the resolution.
10. Within twenty-eight days of the passing of the Special Resolution, any member or members who voted against the resolution may apply to the court for cancellation of the resolution. Notice of Application must be given by the company to the Registrar and a copy of any Court Orders confirming or cancelling the resolution must be delivered to the Registrar within fifteen days of this being made or such other period as the court may order.

Companies House requirements

- Copy of directors' Statutory Declaration. Form G155(6)(a) or (b).
- Copy of auditors' statement pursuant to S156(4).
- Copy of Special Resolution(s).
- Copy of Court Order(s) (if any).

References

The Companies Act 1985 S151–S158 (inclusive).

Redemptions and purchases out of capital

Under certain circumstances private companies may redeem shares or purchase shares out of capital. This is not available to public companies.

The amount of any payment that may be made out of capital is the 'permissible capital payment'. This is defined as the amount of capital together with the proceeds of a fresh issue of shares and also any distributable profit that is required to fund the redemption or purchase.

No payment may be made out of capital unless any retained profits or other distributable reserves have first been applied for this purpose.

Procedure

1. The directors must make a Statutory Declaration specifying the amount of the permissible capital payment and stating that in the directors' opinion:
    (i) the company will be able, immediately following the date of re-purchase or redemption, to pay its debts and,
    (ii) for the following year the company will be able to continue to carry on in business as a going concern and will accordingly be able to pay its debts as they fall due throughout the year.
2. In forming their opinion, the directors must take account of any contingent and prospective liabilities of the company.
3. Attached to the Statutory Declaration by the directors there must be a report to the directors by the auditors of the company stating that they have enquired into the affairs of the company, that the amount specified in the declaration as the permissible capital payment is in their opinion properly calculated and that the auditors are not aware of anything to indicate that the opinion expressed by the directors is unreasonable in the circumstances.
4. The proposed payment out of capital must be approved by Special

Resolution of the shareholders within a week of the date of the Statutory Declaration. The Statutory Declaration and the statement by the auditors of the company must be available for inspection by the members.
5. Within one week of the passing of the Special Resolution the company must give a Public Notice of the payment out of capital and copies of the Statutory Declaration and the Auditors' Report must be filed with the Registrar of Companies no later than the date on which this Notice is given. The Public Notice takes the form of a notice in the *London Gazette* or *Edinburgh Gazette* and either notice in a national newspaper or notice in writing to each of the company's creditors.
6. The Statutory Declaration and the Auditors' Report must be available for inspection at the company's Registered Office for a period of five weeks during which time any member or creditor of the company may apply to the court for an order prohibiting the payment.
7. The payment out of capital may only be made in the fifth, sixth and seventh weeks following the passing of the Special Resolution.

Companies House requirements

- Statutory Declaration by the directors.
- Copy of the auditors' statement.
- Copy of the Special Resolution.
- Copy of the Public Notice.

References

The Companies Act 1985 S171–S177 (inclusive).

Register of Members – rectification

The courts may order rectification of the Register of Members by the removal or addition of a person from or to the Register. Original Orders will bear the seal of the court or, alternatively, a duly authenticated office copy of the Order may be registered.

Procedure

1. The Order should be checked to ensure that the holding referred to corresponds with a registered shareholding in the company – identification will be facilitated by returning the relevant Share Certificate.
2. The amendments authorised in the Order should be made to the Register of Members and the date of the Order and its registration should be entered as the authority for the amendment.
3. The existing Share Certificate may be endorsed as appropriate although it is preferable that a new Share Certificate be prepared.
4. The company's registration stamp should be affixed to the Order which should be returned to the sender together with the endorsed or replacement Share Certificate.
5. If a dividend mandate is currently in force, it may be appropriate for this to be amended, cancelled or renewed.

References

The Companies Act 1985 S359.

Re-registration of a limited company as unlimited

1. The Board of Directors convene an Extraordinary General Meeting to consider resolutions re-registering the company and amending the memorandum and Articles of Association.
2. A notice convening the Extraordinary General Meeting should be issued upon twenty-one clear days notice. Alternatively the meeting may be held upon short notice.
3. At the Extraordinary General Meeting the resolutions will require approval by Special Resolution.

Procedure

1. Application is then made to the Registrar of Companies on form G49(1) together with a copy of the resolution detailing the alterations to the Memorandum and Articles of Association appropriate for an unlimited company.
2. Each member of the company must confirm in writing on form G49(8)(a) that they wish the company to be re-registered as an unlimited company, together with a Statutory Declaration by the Directors that every member has agreed to the re-registration, either personally or by their duly authorised agent. These forms, together with the amendments to the memorandum and Articles of Association, should be submitted to the Registrar together with a fee (currently £50).
3. If accepted, the Registrar issues a new Certificate of Incorporation stating the company's unlimited status whereupon the alterations to the Memorandum and Articles of Association set out in the application take effect. There is no need for the members to pass a Special Resolution approving these amendments.

Notes

Unlimited companies do not normally need to file a copy of their accounts with the Registrar of Companies.

A company which has previously re-registered as Limited from unlimited cannot re-register as unlimited.

Companies House requirements

- Copy of resolutions altering the Memorandum and Articles of Association.
- Amended copy of Memorandum and Articles of Association.
- Declaration by a director that each member has agreed to the re-registration.
- Copy of forms signed by each member. G49(8)(a).
- Re-registration fee (£50; same-day fee £200).
- Form G49(1).

References

The Companies Act 1985 S49, S50.

Re-registration of a private company as a public limited company

Provided that a private limited company can satisfy three conditions it can, by Special Resolution of the shareholders, re-register as a public limited company.

The three conditions are as follows:

1. The issued share capital of the company must have a nominal value of at least £50,000, and each share must be paid up to at least 25 per cent of its nominal value together with all of any premium.
2. The application for re-registration must be received by the Registrar of Companies within seven months of its year end and a copy of an audited balance sheet must be filed on or before the date of application for re-registration. Normally the balance sheet is taken from the usual audited accounts, however, a balance sheet may be submitted made up to an appropriate date not more than seven months prior to the application.
3. The company's auditors must give a statement to the effect that the net assets of the company are not less than its called-up share capital and undistributable reserves and, where the Audit Report to the audited accounts is qualified, that the subject of their qualification is not material for determining that the assets are greater than the called-up share capital and undistributable reserves.

Procedure

1. At a meeting of the Board of Directors the directors should convene an Extraordinary General Meeting to consider the resolutions re-registering the company and amending the Memorandum and Articles of Association. If the company has insufficient share capital, then additional shares must be issued. This is often achieved by a

98 COMPANY SECRETARIAL CHECKLISTS

      Bonus Issue, as a company seeking re-registration will normally have adequate reserves.

2. A notice convening the Extraordinary General Meeting should be issued at least twenty-one clear days before the meeting or, alternatively, the meeting may be held upon short notice.
3. At the Extraordinary General Meeting the appropriate resolutions will require approval by Special Resolution.
4. Within fifteen days of the approval of the Special Resolution the application must be submitted to the Registrar on form 43(3) together with:
   (a) A printed copy of the Memorandum and Articles of Association as altered by the Special Resolution.
   (b) A copy of the statement by the auditors that in their opinion the Balance Sheet shows that the amount of the company's net assets was not less than the aggregate of its called-up share capital and undistributable reserves.
   (c) A copy of the Balance Sheet together with a copy of the unqualified Auditors' Report. If the audit report is qualified, the auditors must certify that the qualification is not material for the purpose of determining the requisite amount of the company's net assets.
   (d) Where appropriate, a copy of a report regarding the valuation of assets taken as payment for shares allotted between the date of the Balance Sheet and the passing of the Special Resolution.
   (e) A Statutory Declaration on form 43(3)(e) stating that the re-registration conditions have been met.

Once the Registrar approves the application he will issue a Certificate of Re-registration at which time the alterations to the Memorandum and Articles take effect.

Notes

There is no obligation for a public company's shares to be quoted. Many private companies re-register for the marketing advantages of being a Plc.

The regulations governing Plcs, the actions of their directors and the preparation of accounts are more onerous than for private companies.

Companies House requirements

- Forms G43(3) and G43(3)(e).

RE-REGISTRATION OF A PRIVATE COMPANY AS PLC

- Copy of relevant Balance Sheet.
- Copy of Audit Report.
- Copy of auditors' statement.
- Copy of amended Memorandum and Articles of Association.
- Copy of Special Resolutions.
- Re-registration fee (£50; same-day fee £200).

References

The Companies Act 1985 S43–S47 (inclusive).

Re-registration of a public limited company as a private limited company

This procedure is rarely encountered in practice as the differences between private and public companies are less marked and it is common for public companies to trade without a stock exchange quotation or a large shareholder base.

Procedure

1. At a meeting of the Board of Directors the directors will convene an Extraordinary General Meeting of the members of the company to approve a Special Resolution that the company be re-registered as a private company. Additionally, resolutions to make certain amendments to the Memorandum and Articles will be required to reflect the company's new status.
2. The notice convening the meeting must be issued to the members at least twenty-one clear days before the meeting or, alternatively, the meeting may be held upon short notice.
3. At the Extraordinary General Meeting the resolutions will require approval by Special Resolution.
4. Within fifteen days a Certified Copy of the Special Resolution must be filed with the Registrar of Companies.
5. Within twenty-eight days of the passing of the resolution an application may be made to the court for the cancellation of the resolution. This application may be made only by a holder or holders of at least 5 per cent of the issued share capital of the company (or of any class of shares) or by not less than fifty of the company's members. If such an application is made, the court may confirm or cancel the resolution or impose certain conditions on its approval. The company must file a copy of any Order made by the court with the Registrar within fifteen days of the making of the Order or within such period as may be determined by the court.

RE-REGISTRATION OF A PLC AS PRIVATE

6. If no application is made to the court within twenty-eight days of the passing of the resolution, an application for re-registration as a private company should be submitted to the Registrar on form 53, signed by a director or secretary, together with a copy of the amended Memorandum and Articles of Association.

Notes

In addition to the voluntary re-registration as a private company, a public company may be *required* to re-register by the court where its issued share capital is below the authorised minimum. This would normally only occur on a reduction of capital or redemption of redeemable shares. In such an event the court may authorise the re-registration to be effective without a Special Resolution being passed and may specify in the Order the amendments to be made to the Memorandum and Articles of Association.

Companies House requirements

- Copy of Special Resolution.
- Form 53.
- Copy of amended Memorandum and Articles of Association.
- Copy of Court Order – if appropriate.
- Re-registration fee (£50; same-day fee £200).

References

The Companies Act 1985 S53–S55 (inclusive).

Re-registration of an unlimited company as a limited company

The members of an unlimited company may re-register the company as limited by Special Resolution.

Procedure

1. The directors in a Board meeting should convene an Extraordinary General Meeting of the shareholders to approve the Special Resolution re-registering the company, amending the memorandum and Articles of Association and detailing how the liability of the members is to be limited (by shares or guarantee).
2. The Extraordinary General Meeting should be convened on twenty-one clear days' notice or, alternatively, the meeting may be convened on short notice.
3. A copy of the resolution should be filed with the Registrar of Companies within fifteen days, together with an application on form 51 and a printed copy of the amended Memorandum and Articles of Association.
4. There is a statutory fee charged by the Registrar of £50.
5. Once accepted by the Registrar, a new Certificate of Incorporation will be issued whereupon the alterations to the Memorandum and Articles of Association will take effect.

Notes

In the circumstances where the company is wound up within three years of re-registration as a limited company, additional protection is given to creditors in respect of debts and liabilities of the company incurred prior to its re-registration.

RE-REGISTRATION OF UNLIMITED COMPANY AS LIMITED

It should be noted that once a company has been re-registered as either unlimited or limited, no further changes to its limited or unlimited status may be made.

Companies House requirements

- Copy of resolutions.
- Amended copy of the Memorandum and Articles of Association.
- Form 51.
- Re-registration fee (£50; same-day fee £200).

References

The Companies Act 1985 S51 and S52.

Re-registration of other companies as public companies

Unlimited companies may also re-register as public limited companies and the procedure is similar to that described on page 97, for private companies.

However, unlimited companies will also have to seek approval for resolutions stating that the liability of the members is to be limited by shares and/or state the amounts of the company's authorised and issued share capital.

Joint stock companies may also be re-registered as public companies by the following procedure:

1. A list of members must be submitted made up to a date not more than six days from the date of re-registration.
2. A copy of the Act or instrument constituting the company.
3. A statement as to the nominal and issued capital and the proposed name of the company.
4. A copy of the resolution that the company be re-registered as a public limited company.
5. A copy of the written statement made in accordance with Section 685(4)(b) of the Companies Act 1985.
6. A copy of the relevant Balance Sheet and unqualified Audit Report by a person qualified to be the company's auditor.
7. A copy of any valuation report concerning the valuation of assets.
8. A Statutory Declaration of compliance by a director or secretary of the company confirming that between the Balance Sheet date and the date of application for re-registration there has been no change in the financial position of the company that has resulted in the company's net assets being less than the aggregate of its called-up capital and undistributable reserves.

Notes

It should be noted that where a joint stock company re-registers as a public limited company and adopts new Articles of Association, if it was originally constituted by an Act of Parliament, Royal Charter or Letters Patent, the existing instruments will continue in force and obviously care must be taken in drafting the Articles of Association to ensure that the provisions of the Articles do not contradict the original constituting instrument.

Companies House requirements

- List of Members.
- A copy of the company's constituting document.
- Statement of authorised and issued share capital.
- Copy of Special Resolution.
- Statement made under S.685.
- Copy of Balance Sheet.
- Copy of Auditors' Report.
- Copy of auditors' statement.
- Copy of any valuations.
- Declaration by a director.
- Re-registration fee (£50; same-day fee £200).

References

The Companies Act 1985 S43–S47 (inclusive) as modified by S48, S51, S680–S690 inclusive.

Related party transactions

Where a director or a person 'connected' with a director acquires a non-cash asset from the company, or disposes of such an asset to the company, in most instances shareholder approval must be sought.

Where the transaction has a value of more than £1,000 and exceeds the lower limit of £50,000 or 10% of the company's net assets, shareholder approval is necessary.

If the director or the connected person is also a director of the company's holding company, then approval of the members of the holding company must also be sought.

Procedure

1. The Board of Directors must convene an Extraordinary General Meeting of the members. The director concerned should also disclose his interest in the matter at this meeting.
2. The Extraordinary General Meeting should be held on fourteen days clear notice. Alternatively the meeting may be held upon short notice.
3. At the Extraordinary General Meeting the resolution should be approved by ordinary resolution.
4. It is not necessary to file a copy with the Registrar of Companies.

Notes

Transactions between companies of a wholly owned group do not require approval.

Where a transaction has not received approval of the members the transaction will usually be voidable by the company.

Transactions undertaken on behalf of the director or connected person on a recognised stock exchange by an 'independent' broker do not require approval.

Where a director acquires a non cash asset by virtue of being a member of the company approval is not required.

Any arrangements entered into which have not received prior approval between a director, connected person or holding company and the company, make that director or connected person liable to the company for any gain arising out of the transaction or any losses suffered by the company.

References

The Companies Act 1985 S320–S322A (inclusive).

Resolutions – filing requirements

A copy of the following resolutions must be filed with the Registrar of Companies within fifteen days of its approval:

1. Special Resolutions.
2. Extraordinary Resolutions.
3. An Elective Resolution or a resolution revoking such a resolution.
4. Resolutions or agreements which have been agreed to by all the members of a company but which, if not so agreed to, would not have been effective for their purpose unless (as the case may be) they had been passed as Special Resolutions or as Extraordinary Resolutions.
5. Resolutions or agreements which have been agreed to by all the members of some class of shareholders but which, if not so agreed to, would not have been effective for their purpose unless they had been passed by some particular majority or otherwise in some particular manner, and all resolutions or agreements which effectively bind all the members of any class of shareholders though not agreed to by all those members.
6. A resolution passed by the directors of a company in compliance with a direction under Section 31(2) (change of name on Secretary of State's direction).
7. A resolution of a company to give, vary, revoke or renew an authority to the directors for the purposes of Section 80 (allotment of relevant securities).
8. A resolution of the directors passed under Section 147(2) (alteration of Memorandum on company ceasing to be a public company, following acquisition of its own shares).
9. A resolution conferring, varying, revoking or renewing authority under Section 166 (market purchase of company's own shares).

RESOLUTIONS – FILING REQUIREMENTS

10. A resolution for voluntary winding up, passed under Section 84(1)(a),(b) or (c) of the Insolvency Act 1986.
11. A resolution increasing a company's authorised share capital.

References

The Companies Act 1985 S123, S380.

Resolutions – majority

The majorities required to pass resolutions are as follows:

1. Ordinary Resolutions   simple majority
2. Extraordinary Resolutions   75% majority
3. Special Resolutions   75% majority
4. Elective Resolutions   100% majority

The majority for Ordinary, Extraordinary or Special Resolutions is of those members entitled to attend and vote *and* present and voting at a general meeting in person or by proxy.

The Elective Resolution requires unanimous approval of all members entitled to attend and vote, *whether or not* such members attend a general meeting convened for the purpose.

References

The Companies Act 1985 S378, S379A.

Resolutions in writing

The Companies Act 1989 has introduced into statute the principle that the members of the company may, by Written Resolution of all the shareholders, pass resolutions which would otherwise require a general meeting to be held.

Resolutions in Writing of all the members have long been accepted as good practise and binding on the company and the Companies Act 1989 clarifies and gives statutory authority to this practice.

Resolutions of the Board of Directors are also acceptable if due authority is contained in the company's Articles of Association.

Written Resolutions must be signed by or on behalf of all the members of the company or where approval is sought of any particular class of members, from those members who at the date of the resolution are entitled and attend and vote at such a class.

The signatures need not all appear on the same document, provided that all the signed documents are in the same form, the resolution is effective and dated when signed by or on behalf of the last member to sign.

A copy of all proposed Written Resolutions must be sent to the company's auditors. If the resolution concerns the auditors in their capacity as auditors, they may within seven days give notice to the company that in their opinion the matter should be considered at a meeting of the members.

Any Written Resolution does not have effect until a period of seven days elapses without any notice being given by the auditors to the company or the auditors informing the company that the particular resolution does not concern them as auditors or that it does concern them as auditors but that they do not consider that a meeting need be held.

The original signed copies of the Written Resolution should be inserted in the company's Minute Book in the normal manner.

There are two resolutions that cannot be passed by a Written Resolution under any circumstances:

1. The removal of a director pursuant to Section 303 of the Companies Act 1985 before the expiration of his period of office.
2. The removal of an auditor under Section 391 of the Companies Act 1985 before the expiration of his period of office.

As the majority of resolutions may now be passed by Resolutions in Writing, certain changes have been necessitated to the circulation of documentation to shareholders. Accordingly, documents which are required to be circulated to shareholders with a notice of a general meeting or are to be made available at the company's Registered Office for inspection prior to the meeting must, where a Written Resolution is to be used, be circulated to each member before or at the same time as the resolution is supplied for signature. Such documents include the following:

1. A written statement to be given by directors pursuant to a Special Resolution, waiving the rights of pre-emption on the allotment of shares.
2. The Statutory Declaration and Auditors' Report relating to an approval for financial assistance by a company for the purchase of its shares.
3. A copy of the purchase contract, or written memorandum of its terms relating to the off-market purchase or contingent purchase by a company of its own shares.
4. A Statutory Declaration and Auditors' Report relating to the purchase by a company of its own shares out of capital.
5. A written memorandum setting out the terms of a proposed director's service contract for a term of more than five years.
6. Disclosure of matters relating to the approval of a director's expenditure to enable him properly to perform his duties.

Where any particular member is interested in the matter to be approved by Written Resolution and he would not be eligible to vote at a general meeting, he is similarly barred from voting by Written Resolution on the same matter.

Where the resolutions would have had to be passed by Special or Extraordinary Resolution at a meeting and a copy of the resolution is required to be filed with the Registrar of Companies, a copy of the Written Resolution must be filed in its place. In addition where a copy of an ordinary resolution must be filed with the Registrar of Companies a copy of the Written Resolution must be filed.

Companies House requirements

- Copies of Written Resolutions as appropriate (see page 108).

References

The Companies Act 1985 S381A, S381B, S381C, S382A, and Schedule 15A.

Restoration

Where a company has been dissolved and struck off the Register pursuant to Section 652 of the Companies Act 1985, the directors, shareholders or under certain circumstances creditors of the company may apply to have the company restored to the Register.

Application is made to a county court.

Prior to restoration it will be necessary to bring the company's statutory records up to date and this will normally involve the completion of all outstanding Annual Returns and the preparation of audited accounts as well as any changes in shareholdings, officers or other statutory details of the company to be filed.

In addition to the restoration fee payable to the Registrar of Companies (currently £200), the company will also be required to pay the legal costs of the Registrar, and the penalties for late submission of accounts – as appropriate.

Notes

In practice restoration is often required where a company has been dissolved by the Registrar (for failure to file returns and/or accounts) or at the request of the Directors/Shareholders and it is subsequently found that the company has valuable assets. In these circumstances, it is necessary for the company to be restored to the register for the assets to be reclaimed, as the assets of a dissolved company automatically attach to the crown. It is becoming increasingly common for a company with assets to be dissolved as a result of oversight on the part of Directors; either neglect in filing statutory documents, or requesting the Director to strike off the company without properly checking that the company has no assets. For example, particular care should be taken when requesting the dissolution of a subsidiary that the legal ownership of property has passed to its holding company or fellow subsidiary. It is not uncommon for the appropriate book entries to be made, for example, transferring the lease of a property to another group company without ensuring that the legal transfer of title is also effected.

Occasionally a company which has been dissolved will be found to have a large outstanding creditor. In such circumstances the creditor may apply to the court to have the company restored to the Register at the company's cost, to enable him to pursue his claim.

References

The Companies Act 1985 S653, S654.

Rights Issue

A Rights Issue is an issue of shares to the existing shareholders pro rata to their existing holdings.

Rights Issues are used by companies to obtain additional funding from the company's shareholders rather than obtaining working capital by borrowing from banks or other financial institutions.

Procedure

1. The Articles of Association must be checked to ensure that the company has sufficient unissued authorised share capital and that the directors have been authorised in terms of Section 80 of the Companies Act 1985 to allot additional shares. If the company has insufficient share capital, it will be necessary to increase the company's share capital (see page 26).
2. The directors should resolve to increase the company's issued share capital by way of a Rights Issue and resolve to issue the provisional allotment letters to the company's shareholders.

    If it is intended that the existing shareholders may renounce their entitlement to third parties, these letters include letters of renunciation.
3. Once the closing date for the acceptance of the allotment letters has been reached, the directors will meet to allot those shares taken up.
4. The secretary should ensure that appropriate Share Certificates are prepared and issued to the shareholders and that a form G88(2) is filed with the Registrar of Companies within fifteen days.
5. The secretary should ensure that the Register of Members is written up to reflect the issue of shares.

RIGHTS ISSUE 117

Notes

If the Rights Issue is to be made by way of Renounceable Letters of Allotment the Articles of Association must be checked to ensure that no pre-emption rights on allotment are infringed.

To the extent that such rights may be infringed the procedures on page 84 should be followed.

Companies House requirements

- Form G88(2).
- Copies of any Ordinary and Special Resolutions and form G123 as necessary.

References

The Companies Act 1985 S80, S88–S91, S95.

Secretary – appointment

The person named as secretary on form G10 delivered with the Memorandum and Articles of Association for registration is deemed to have been appointed as secretary upon incorporation.

Subsequent appointments of secretaries are made by the Board of Directors in accordance with the provisions contained in the company's Articles of Association.

Procedure

1. The directors at a meeting of the Board of Directors will resolve to appoint a new company secretary in place of a resigning secretary or one who is to be removed.
2. A form G288 must be filed with the Registrar of Companies within fourteen days of the date of appointment.
3. The necessary entry must be made in the Register of Secretaries.
4. The company secretary is frequently a signatory on the company's bank account and accordingly it may be necessary to amend the company's bank Mandate in addition to notifying the bank of the new appointment and supplying specimen signatures to the bank.
5. The Board will normally consider it necessary for the company secretary to have a service contract.
6. If the company secretary is to carry out executive duties, it may be considered necessary to include the company secretary on any policy of directors' and officers' indemnity insurance.

Notes

It should be noted that the company's auditors, in addition to being disbarred from acting as directors of the company, may not be the company secretary.

The appointment of a company secretary may be terminated by the directors. There is no need for shareholder approval. The secretary may be able to bring an action for breach of contract in such circumstances.

Companies House requirements

- Form G288 – Appointment and resignation.

References

The Companies Act 1985 S10, S13, S283, S286, S288.

Secretary – duties

Neither of the Companies Acts nor the Articles of Association stipulate in any detail the duties of the company secretary. However, the secretary is named as one of the persons who may sign prescribed forms and is an 'officer' of the company in terms of Section 744 of the Companies Act 1985.

Although the secretary has no specific statutory duties the following are normally dealt with by the company secretary:

1. Maintenance of statutory registers:
   (a) Register of Members.
   (b) Register of Charges.
   (c) Minute Books – Shareholders and Directors.
   (d) Register of Directors and Secretaries.
   (e) Register of Directors' interests.
   (f) Register of debentures/stockholders – if appropriate.
2. Completion of statutory forms (see page 148) as necessary, the most common forms being:
   (a) Annual Return.
   (b) Changes in directors or secretaries.
   (c) Change in registered office.
   (d) Allotment of shares.
   (e) Increases or changes in share capital.
3. Authenticating company documentation.
4. Issue of share certificates and loan stock certificates as appropriate.
5. To ensure the safe keeping of:
   The company seal and the company's copies of documentation including:
   (a) Directors' service contracts.
   (b) Leases in respect of the company's property.
   (c) Agreements, leases for office equipment, etc.

(d) Documents of Title including share certificates, stock transfer forms, etc.
6. As chief administrative officer the secretary will often deal with:
   (a) Employment of staff.
   (b) Contracts relating to the company's premises and office equipment.
   (c) The company's printing and stationery requirements.
   (d) The company pension arrangements and employee share option schemes.
   (e) Company cars.
   (f) Management accounting.

Where the company secretary is not also a director of the company he would not normally be involved in contracts and agreements relating to the company's trading activities.

The secretary should attend and take minutes of meetings of the board of directors and of shareholders. The secretary at the request of the chairman of the directors or of individual directors will convene meetings of the directors and shareholders. The secretary should advise the board of directors on technical compliance matters relating to the companies acts and other related issues.

There are many other areas in which company secretaries can and often do become involved relating to the management of companies. However, as this book is directed towards the company law compliance aspects of a company secretary's role these additional roles are not listed here. For a more comprehensive list readers should direct their enquiries to the Institute of Chartered Secretaries and Administrators who have issued a guide entitled 'The Duties of the Company Secretary'.

Sensitive words

Certain words and phrases ('sensitive' words) will require either the consent of the Secretary of State for Trade and Industry before their use will be allowed in a company name alternatively the Secretary of State may require that appropriate authority be obtained from a relevant body.

The sensitive words that require the consent of the Secretary of State for Trade and Industry are:

1. Words which imply national or international pre-eminence.
2. Words which imply governmental patronage or sponsorship.
3. Words which imply business pre-eminence or representative status.
4. Words which imply specific objects or functions.

For a company to use one or more of these words in its name, its use must be justified.

The Registrar of Companies has issued guidelines giving details of the criteria to be used and these are set out below. It should be noted, however, that these are not definitive criteria and in every case the decision on whether or not to allow a particular name to be used will rest with the Secretary of State for Trade and Industry.

Words which imply national or international pre-emimence.

British. The criteria for this word can vary according to the way in which it is used in the name. Normally, ownership should be British, and the company must show pre-eminence in its field preferably by independent support, e.g. from the Government, Parliament or appropriate trade association. If 'British' is qualified by words not describing an activity or product, i.e. by a made-up word, pre-eminence is not necessarily essential, but the company should be substantial in the context of its activities and eminent within its field.

National. The criteria are similar to 'British' (above) and the company should show evidence of trading throughout the United Kingdom.

Great Britain, United Kingdom. If used as a prefix or preceded with the word 'of', will be treated as for 'British'.

England, English, Scotland, Scottish, Wales, Welsh, Ireland, Irish. These will be treated as for 'British' when used as prefixes. When used as a suffix, the name will normally be approved, provided the company is trading in their relevant country. If used as surnames, the names will be approved if coupled with initials or forenames.

International. As a prefix, the company must be substantial in the context of its activities and trade in overseas countries. As a suffix, it will be generally approved where it can be shown that the company's main activities are export, or that it operates in more than one overseas country. When linked to a trade or service which is international in character, e.g. travel, transport, etc., it may be approved, provided it is not too pretentious or likely to give rise to justified complaint.

European. The name is mainly approved if it does not imply connection with the European Community, and provided the name as a whole is not too pretentious or likely to give rise to justified complaint.

Words which imply governmental or public authority patronage or sponsorship.

Authority, Board, Council. If the name implies governmental or public authority, patronage or sponsorshp, evidence should be supplied, e.g. a letter of support and consent from a relevant body.

Words which imply business pre-eminence or representative status.

Association, Federation, Society. The company should normally be limited by guarantee, controlled by members and non-profit distributing.

Institute, Institution. Normally only approved to organisations carrying out research at the highest level or to professional bodies of the highest standing. The company must show that it does not conflict with other existing organisations, has appropriate examinations or regulations, and evidence of support from other representative and independent bodies. Companies proposing to use these names should contact the Department of Trade and Industry for further information.

Words which imply specific objects or functions.

Insurance Words, i.e. Insurance, Re-Insurance, Insurer, Assurer, Re-Assurer, Re-Insurer. If a name is required for an underwriting company, the department will normally seek further advice. If the company is only to provide insurance services, i.e. agents, consultants, etc., the name should be qualified by the addition of the appropriate words.

Patent, Patentee. The names will only be approved if they do not contravene the Patents Act.

Chamber of Commerce, Trade, Industry, etc. The department will seek advice from the Association of British Chambers of Commerce.

Co-operative. The company should be limited by guarantee with control in the hands of members and distribution of any profits controlled. More detailed information may be required before names with this word can be approved.

Group. When used in the sense that there are a number of companies under one ownership, then association with two or more British or overseas companies should be shown. If the name clearly shows that the company is to provide the interests of a collection of individuals, i.e. computer software user group, it will be approved.

Holdings. The company should be a holding company within the terms of Section 736 of the Companies Act 1985.

Post Office, Giro. The Department may seek advice on applications.

Trust. 'Trust' can be used in many senses and different criteria will apply. The notes below cover the main uses of this word but there may be others which will have to be dealt with on an individual basis.

 Financial and investment trusts. These require a written assurance that substantial paid-up share capital or other funds will be achieved within a reasonable period of incorporation.

 Family trusts. The name will be allowed, provided the rest of the name identifies it as such. The company should be non-profit distributing and the objects reflect the nature of the trust.

 Education or Artistic Trusts. These should have a non-profit distribution clause, the promoters should be of some standing in their field and the name reflect the nature of the trust.

 Charitable Trusts. These require charitable objects, a non-profit distribution clause and confirmation that an application has or will be made for registration with the Charity Commission.

SENSITIVE WORDS 125

Pensions and Staff Trusts. These should include the name of the parent company, and objects should include the operation of the pension funds.

Enterprise Trusts. These should have a non-profit distribution clause and recognisable support, i.e. from local authorities, businesses, banks. Use of the words **'unit trusts'** will require Departmental approval.

Stock Exchange. This will normally be refused unless there are special circumstances.

Register, Registered. If these words are linked with a professional qualification, advice may be sought from the appropriate body. The name should not imply connection with Her Majesty's Government or a local authority.

Building Society, Friendly Society and Industrial Provident Society. Names including these words will be referred to the Registrar of Friendly Societies for advice.

Trade Union. Names including these words will not normally be approved unless they conform to legislation relating to trade unions.

Charter, Chartered. Names including these words will be refused if they give a false impression that the company has a Royal Charter. If used to qualify a profession, advice of the appropriate governing body will be sought.

Sheffield. If the name implies connection with the traditional Sheffield industries, advice of the Cutlers Company will be sought.

Benevolent, Foundation, Fund. If the name implies charitable status, it will not normally be approved unless the company is limited by guarantee and is non-profit distributing.

Chemist, Chemistry. The advice of Companies Registration Office should be sought about the use of these words in names.

The following schedule details words the use of which will only be allowed if the applicant has obtained a letter of non-objection from the relevant department or body. Any such correspondence should be submitted with the appropriate registration or change of name and documentation.

126 COMPANY SECRETARIAL CHECKLISTS

Word or expression	Relevant body for companies incorporated in England or Wales	Relevant body for companies registered in Scotland
Royal, Royale, Royalty, King, Queen, Prince, Princess, Windsor, Duke, His Majesty, Her Majesty	E2 Division (Room 29), Home Office, Queen Anne Gate, London SW1H 9AT	The Scottish Home and Health Department, Old St Andrew's House, Edinburgh EH1 3DE
District Nurse, Health Visitor, Midwife, Midwifery, Nurse	Principal Administrative Officer, English National Board for Nursing, Midwifery and Health Visiting, Victory House, 170 Tottenham Court Road, London W1P 0HA	The Registrar, National Board for Nursing, Midwifery and Health Visiting, 22 Queen Street, Edinburgh EH2 1JX
Health Centre	Division PMC1 (c), Room B1205, Department of Health and Social Security, Alexander Fleming House, Elephant and Castle, London SE1 6TE	As for England and Wales
Health Service	HS2D Division (Room 1115), Department of Health and Social Security, Hannibal House, Elephant and Castle, London SE1 6TE	As for England and Wales
Nursing Home	H43A Division (Room 1221), Department of Health and Social Security, Hannibal House, Elephant and Castle, London SE1 6TE	As for England and Wales

SENSITIVE WORDS 127

Pregnancy, Termination, Abortion	PMC2A Division (Room B1210), Department of Health and Social Security, Alexander Fleming House, Elephant and Castle, London SE1 6TE	As for England and Wales
Breed, Breeder	Animal Health III Division, Ministry of Agriculture, Fisheries and Food, Tolworth Tower, Surbiton, Surrey KT6 7DX	As for England and Wales
Charity, Charitable	Registration Division, Charities Commission, St Alban's House, 57–60 Haymarket, London SW1Y 4QX	Civil Law and Charities Division, Scottish Home and Health Department, St Andrew's House, Edinburgh EH1 3DE
Apothecary	The Worshipful Society of Apothecaries of London, Apothecaries Hall, Black Friars Lane, London EC4	The Pharmaceutical Society of Great Britain, 1 Lambeth High Street, London SE1 7JN
University, Polytechnic	FHE3, Department of Education and Science, Elizabeth House, York Road, London SE1 7PH	As for England and Wales
Police	F1 Division, Police Department, Home Office, Queen Anne Gate, London SW1H 9AT	Police Division, The Scottish Home and Health Department, Old St Andrew's House, Edinburgh EH1 3DE
Special School	School RN11 Branch, Department of Education and Science, Elizabeth House, York Road, London SE1 7PH	As for England and Wales

Contact Lens	The Registrar, General Optical Council, 41 Harley Street, London W1N 2DJ	As for England and Wales
Dental, Dentistry	The Registrar, General Dental Council, 37 Wimpole Street, London W1M 8DQ	As for England and Wales

The use of certain words in a company's name is covered by legislation other than the Companies Act 1985. The schedule below sets out details of the words, the relevant legislation and the relevant body from which authorisation should be sought.

Word or expression	Relevant legislation	Relevant body
Architect, Architectural	Section 1, Architects Registration Act 1938	The Registrar, Architects Registration Council of the United Kingdom, 73 Hallener Street, London W1N 6EE.
Credit Union	Credit Union Act 1979	Registrar of Friendly Societies, 15 – 17 Great Marlborough Street, London W1V 2AX
Veterinary Surgeon	Sections 19 and 20, Veterinary Surgeons Act 1966	The Registrar, Royal College of Veterinary Surgeons, 32 Belgrave Square, London SW1X 8QP
Dentist, Dental Surgeon, Dental Practitioner	Dentist Act 1984	The Registrar-General, Dental Council, 37 Wimpole Street, London W1M 8DQ

Drug, Druggist, Pharmaceutical, Pharmaceutist, Pharmacist, Pharmacy	Section 78, Medicines Act 1978	Head of the Law Department, The Pharmaceutical Society of Great Britain, 1 Lambeth High Street, London SE1 7JN
Optician, Ophthalmic Optician, Dispensing Optician, Enrolled Optician, Registered Optician, Optometrist	Sections 4 and 22, Opticians Act 1958 and Health and Social Security Act 1984	The Registrar, General Optical Council, 41 Harley Street, London W1N 2DJ
Bank, Banker, Banking Deposit	Banking Act 1979	Bank of England, Threadneedle Street, London EC2R 8AH
Red Cross	Geneva Convention Act 1957	Liaise with Companies House
Anzac	Section 1, Anzac Act 1916	Liaise with Companies House
Insurance Broker, Assurance Broker, Re-Insurance Broker, Re-Assurance Broker	Sections 2 and 3, Insurance Brokers (Registration) Acts 1977	Liaise with Companies House
Chiropodist, Dietitian, Medical Laboratory Technician, Occupational Therapist, Orthoptist, Physiotherapist, Radiographer, Remedial Gymnast	Profession Supplementary to Medicines Act 1960 (if preceded by Registered or State)	Room 77, Department of Health and Social Security, Hanover House, Elephant and Castle, London SE1 6TE

Share Certificate – duplicate

In the event of a shareholder losing their Share Certificate the following procedure should be followed:

1. The shareholder should be sent a Form of Indemnity in respect of the issue of a duplicate certificate. This is to protect the company should the original Share Certificate fall into the wrong hands and an attempt be made to fraudulently transfer the shares.
2. The Form of Indemnity should be signed by the shareholder and for most quoted public limited companies it will be necessary for the indemnity to be guaranteed by a bank or insurance company.
3. On receipt by the company of a completed Indemnity Form a duplicate Share Certificate should be prepared and issued to the shareholder.
4. If the original Share Certificate is found, it should be returned to the company and cancelled.

Shareholders – Power of Attorney

Where a Power of Attorney is received for registration, the following procedure should be maintained:

1. The document received for registration must be the original document bearing a 50p stamp duty impression, or an authenticated copy of it.
2. Care must be taken to ensure that the person granting the Power of Attorney is indeed a member of the company and holds the appropriate number of shares. It may be that the Power of Attorney is being granted by a member who has only recently acquired shares either by allotment, renunciation of Bonus or Rights Issue or by transfer.
3. A copy of the Power of Attorney should be retained by the company for its records.
4. The terms of the Power of Attorney must be checked to see whether one attorney is being appointed or more than one. In the case of more than one attorney, it will be necessary to check whether one attorney acting on his own has power to effect transfers or whether all attorneys must act together.
5. The Power of Attorney may change the registered address for the shareholder and the matter of to whom any future dividends must be made.
6. If the Power of Attorney is in order, the company's registration stamp should be affixed to the original document and it should be returned to the person giving the Power of Attorney.
7. On every occasion that documents are executed by the Attorney this should be cross-referenced with the copy of the Power of Attorney retained by the company to ensure that the terms of the Power of Attorney have been complied with.
8. Neither the name in the Register of Members nor the original Share Certificate require amendment since the beneficial owner is not

changing and, indeed, as the Register is a public document the appointment of a Power of Attorney should not be noted on it.
9. A Power of Attorney can be revoked or changed by the person giving the Power of Attorney at any time or, alternatively, the Power of Attorney may be given for a specific occasion or for a specific length of time.

Shareholders – Probate

A company should accept for registration any Grant of Probate for confirmation, or a properly validated copy, provided that it bears the court seal.

Procedure

A careful check must be made to ensure that the details shown on the Grant of Probate correspond with the entry in the Register of Members. If there is any doubt as to whether the deceased is indeed a shareholder of the company, then the company should obtain a Declaration of Identity from the executors. This will usually be given by the solicitors acting for the Estate, although the deceased's bankers can also give a Declaration of Identity.

Details of the Probate should be recorded in the company's Document Register.

The date of death and the date of registration of the Probate together with the name(s) and address(es) of the executor(s) should be noted in the Register of Members and the Register should be amended to show the word 'deceased' after the shareholder's name. The postal address for correspondence should be amended to that of the executor and should be addressed to the 'Executor of [shareholder's name] deceased'.

The Share Certificates should be endorsed with fact and date of death, the date of registration of Probate and the name(s) and address(es) of the executor(s). The endorsement should be validated with the company's security seal.

The company's security seal should be impressed on the Probate and the Probate together with the amended Share Certificate should be returned to the person who lodged them. A new dividend mandate form may also be enclosed as any existing mandate will have been revoked on the death of the shareholder.

The company may request that the executor(s) transfer the shares to themselves as this simplifies further requests and the need to validate instructions no longer applies. This transfer may, however, invoke the pre-emption provisions contained in the Articles of Association.

References

The Companies Act 1985 S187.

Shares – application and allotment

Procedure

1. Prior to the issue, the directors should ensure that they have sufficient authority to allot shares and that pre-emption provisions on the allotment of shares contained in the company's Articles of Association are not infringed or to the extent that they are that the necessary waivers have been received from the members, either in writing or in general meeting (see page 84).
2. If the company does not have sufficient unissued shares, it will be necessary to convene an Extraordinary General Meeting of the shareholders to increase the authorised share capital, increase the directors' authority to allot shares and, if necessary, to waive the pre-emption rights contained in the Articles of Association.
3. A form of application should be made available for those persons wishing to subscribe for shares. Private companies must take care when drafting an application letter to make sure that it is not regarded as an invitation to the public to subscribe for shares. Only public companies can issue shares to the public.
4. Those persons wishing to subscribe for the shares will complete the application form and return this to the company together with a cheque in full or part payment for the shares, as appropriate.
5. Once the application forms and remittances have been received, the remittance cheques should be banked as soon as possible.
6. The Board of Directors should pass a resolution to allot the shares, to authorise the issue of Share Certificates and to authorise the entry of the new holding in the company's Register of Members.
7. As soon as possible, Share Certificates should be issued to the applicants and in any event not more than two months from the date of allotment.

136 COMPANY SECRETARIAL CHECKLISTS

8. Within one month of the date of allotment a Return of Allotments (form G88(2)) should be filed with the Registrar of Companies.
9. If the shares are all fully paid, it will not be necessary for the shares to have distinguishing numbers.

Notes

For allotments for a non-cash consideration or Bonus Issue see page 30.

Under certain circumstances fully paid and partly paid shares of the same class may be regarded as two different classes of shares.

Companies House requirements

- Form G88(2) within fifteen days.
- Form G88(3) – if shares paid otherwise than in cash.

References

The Companies Act 1985 SS80–S107 inclusive.

Shares – consolidation

Occasionally, it will be necessary to consolidate the share capital of the company into shares of a greater nominal value. For instance, a consolidation of 4,000 25p shares into £1.00 shares will result in the authorised share capital being 1,000 shares of £1.00 each.

Occasionally, a quoted public limited company will consolidate its shares into shares of a higher nominal value where the shares have a very low market price. The consolidation of the shares will effectively increase the market price and make it easier to trade in the shares.

Alternatively, consolidation of shares will be used in capital reconstruction or capital reduction schemes. For instance, a company may decide to reduce its capital from £1.00 shares to 50p shares and then consolidate the shares into £1.00 shares, thus achieving a 50 per cent capital reduction whilst retaining a nominal value of £1.00 for the shares.

Procedure

1. The directors should convene a meeting of the shareholders of the company to approve an Ordinary Resolution consolidating the shares. The shareholders would also need to authorise the directors to sell any fractions of shares arising on consolidation for the benefit of the members entitled to them.
2. The secretary should issue appropriate notice and proxy forms and ensure that a venue is available for the meeting. The resolutions to be passed are Ordinary Resolutions and require 50 per cent majority. As these are Ordinary Resolutions it will not be necessary to file a copy of the resolutions with the Registrar of Companies, although it will be necessary to file a form 122 detailing the consolidation to the Registrar within one month from the date of the resolution being passed.

3. The Register of Members will require amendment to show details of the new number of shares and nominal value of the shares currently held and any distinguishing numbers will require re-allocation.
4. If there are any fractions of shares arising upon the consolidation, these should be sold for the benefit of the members concerned or, alternatively, occasionally new shares can be issued, credited as fully paid, to round their holding up to the nearest whole number.
5. All existing Share Certificates should be recalled, either for amendment or cancellation, new Share Certificates being issued.

Companies House requirements

- Form 122.

Shares – convertible

As the name implies, these are shares which can be converted from one class to another, either at some specific time in the future, on the occurrence of a specific event or at the option of the company or the shareholder.

Convertible Shares will often be issued so that the company can attract additional funds, with the shares being issued with enhanced dividend rights. After a period of time, the shares would be converted to Ordinary Shares, thus reducing the dividends payable by the company.

In many ways the issue of Convertible Shares is similar to loans to the company but with repayment of the loan at the end of its term being replaced by conversion to Ordinary Shares.

The following points should be considered when Convertible Shares are being created:

1. Whether the shares could carry pre-emption rights on allotment or transfer.
2. The amount, if any, of dividend and whether this should be preferential.
3. Whether the shares should carry voting rights.
4. Whether the shares should carry a preferential right to the return of capital on any winding up or distribution and whether the shares should participate in any surplus.
5. The terms of conversion, including whether conversion should be at the option of the company, the shareholder or both, or at predetermined dates, and the basis of conversion to Ordinary Shares.
6. Creation of the shares will require alterations to the Articles of Association and to the authorised share capital and must be authorised by the shareholders by Ordinary and Special Resolutions at a general meeting.

140 COMPANY SECRETARIAL CHECKLISTS

7. Once the shares have been created any further changes to the Articles of Association may require approval of the holders of the Convertible Shares at a separate class meeting, whether or not they are voting shares.
8. The company should maintain sufficient unissued authorised share capital of the class of shares into which the Convertible Shares will be converted and will require authority from the shareholders to issue the shares.
9. The procedure to be followed on conversion of the shares is the same as that to be followed on the conversion of convertible loan stock (see page 74).

References

The Companies Act 1985 S80–S88 (inclusive).

Shares – cumulative

The dividend payable on such shares is 'cumulative', that is any dividend not paid on the shares in one year will be accumulated and paid in succeeding years.

As dividends can only be paid out of distributable profits available for the purpose, the dividend may not be paid in a particular year as the company has insufficient distributable profit. In these circumstances the unpaid dividend will accumulate until such time as the company has sufficient distributable profit to pay a dividend and any arrears to date.

It would be unusual for cumulative shares not to have a fixed dividend, as the directors would only declare a discretionary dividend in the circumstances where the company has profits available for distribution.

The following points should be considered when cumulative shares are being created:

1. Whether the shares should carry pre-emption rights on allotment or transfer.
2. Whether the shares will have a preferential right to the return of capital and whether this should be limited to the amounts paid up or credited as paid up on the shares or whether they should participate in any surplus.
3. Whether the shares should be voting shares.
4. The amount of the fixed dividend and any preferential payment terms, i.e. before or after any dividend to be declared on any other class of shares.
5. The creation of the shares will require alterations to the Articles of Association and to the authorised share capital of the company. If the shares are to be created after the incorporation of the company, the creation of the shares will require the consent of the shareholders by Ordinary and Special Resolutions at an Extraordinary General Meeting.

142 COMPANY SECRETARIAL CHECKLISTS

6. Any subsequent alteration to the Articles may also require approval of the holders of any cumulative shares if the alteration alters their class rights. This approval will be required at a separate class meeting and is required even where the particular class of shares are non-voting.
7. Whether or not the shares should be redeemable or convertible at some future date.

References

The Companies Act 1985 S80–S88 (inclusive).

Shares – redeemable

A limited company having a share capital may, if authorised by its Articles of Association, issue shares which are redeemable or which are liable to be redeemed at the option of the company or the shareholder.

Procedure

At the time of issue of redeemable shares there must be in issue shares which are not redeemable. This is to ensure that the issued share capital of the company cannot all be redeemed, leaving the company with no shareholders.

Redeemable shares can only be redeemed if they are fully paid.

The terms of redemption must provide for payment in cash on redemption.

Redeemable shares may only be redeemed out of the distributable profits or out of the proceeds of a fresh issue of shares made for that purpose. Under certain circumstances private companies may redeem shares out of capital.

Redeemed shares are treated as cancelled on redemption, the amount of the issued share capital being reduced by the nominal value of the shares.

Companies House requirements

- Form G122.

References

The Companies Act 1985 S122, S159–S170 (inclusive).

Shares – transfer

Procedure

1. The transferor should complete a stock transfer form giving details of the shares to be transferred, their own name and address as transferor and the name and address of the transferee. The form should be signed by the transferor and, where the shares are partly paid, by the transferee.
2. Prior to registration by the company it will be necessary for the stock transfer form to be stamped by the Inland Revenue unless the transfer is exempt from duty and has been signed and certified on the reverse. Stamp duty is payable by the purchaser of the shares. The current rate for stamp duty is 0.5 per cent of the consideration paid or payable (whether or not the consideration is cash). Certain transfers are subject to a fixed duty of 50p.
3. The stamped stock transfer form together with the original Share Certificate should be forwarded to the company or its registrar (as appropriate) for registration.
4. Upon receipt of a stock transfer form the company should check that the details of the transferor are correct and that the Share Certificate is valid. If the original Share Certificate has become mislaid, it will be necessary for the transferor to complete an indemnity in respect of this lost certificate.
5. Many private companies have detailed pre-emption provisions on the transfer of shares and care must be taken to ensure that these are followed. Alternatively, the pre-emption rights may be waived by the remaining shareholders.
6. The transfer of shares requires approval from the Board of Directors who should also authorise the issue of a Share Certificate to the transferee and of any balancing certificate to the transferrer.
7. Details of the transfer must be entered in the Register of Members.

Notes

Share transfers are not notified to Companies House; however, details of the transfer must be shown on the company's next Annual Return.

References

The Companies Act 1985 S182–S186 (inclusive).

Single member companies

With effect from 15 July 1992 private companies limited by shares or by guarantee may be incorporated with one member and existing companies may reduce their membership to one. These provisions are contained in the Companies (Single Member Private Limited Companies) Regulations 1992 No. 1699.

Where any person has by virtue of section 24 of the Companies Act 1985 become liable for the payment of any debts of a private company limited by shares or by guarantee that person will not be liable for any debts contracted after 15 July 1992, but will remain liable for any debts incurred prior to that date.

The regulations introduced a number of procedures to be followed by single member companies:

1. Where a private company limited by shares or by guarantee having only one member enters into a contract with a sole member of the company and the sole member is also a director of the company, the company shall, unless the contract is in writing, ensure that the terms of the contract are set out in a written memorandum or are recorded in the minutes of the first meeting of the directors of the company following the making of the contract. This provision will, however, not apply to contracts entered into in the ordinary course of the company's business.
2. When a private company has only one member the following must be entered in the Register of Members with the details of the sole member:
   (a) A statement that the company only has one member.
   (b) The date on which the company became a single member company.
3. When the membership of a single member company increases then the following details must be added to the details of the former single member:

(a) A statement that the company has ceased to be a single member company.
(b) The date the company ceased to be a single member company.
4. Notwithstanding any provision in the Company's Articles of Association the quorum for meetings of the members of a single member company shall be one.
5. The single member must provide the company with a written record of all resolutions that have been passed in 'general meeting'.

Notes

These provisions have been introduced as part of the general harmonisation of company law throughout the EEC.

It will no longer be necessary for one share to be held by a nominee on behalf of the holding company or the 'sole' owner of a company.

The sole director of the company, whether single member or not, is still prohibited from also being the company secretary.

References

The Companies (Single Member Private Limited Companies) Regulations 1992.

The Companies Act 1985 S3A, S322B, S370A, S382B.

Statutory forms and filing periods

Form No.	Description	Filing period
6	Notice of application to the court for cancellation of alteration to the objects of a company	15 days of notice
10	Statement of first directors and secretary and intended situation of Registered Office	Required for incorporation
12	Statutory Declaration of compliance with requirements on application for registration of a company	Required for incorporation
30(5)a	Declaration on application for the registration of a company exempt from the requirement to use the word 'limited' (or its Welsh equivalent)	With form 10
30(5)5b	Declaration on application for registration under S.680, CA 1985 of a company exempt from the requirement to use the word 'limited' (or its Welsh equivalent)	With form 630
30(5)c	Declaration on change of name omitting 'limited' (or its Welsh equivalent)	With change-of-name resolution
43(3)	Application by a private company for re-registration as a public company	15 days
43(3)(e)	Declaration of compliance with the requirements by a private company for re-registration as a public company	15 days
49(1)	Application by a limited company to be re-registered as unlimited	15 days

STATUTORY FORMS AND FILING PERIODS

Form No.	Description	Filing period
49(8)(a)	Members' assent to company being re-registered as unlimited	15 days
51	Application by an unlimited company to be re-registered as limited	15 days
53	Application by a public company for re-registration as a private company	After 28 days
54	Notice of application made to the court for the cancellation of a Special Resolution regarding re-registration	On notice
88(2)	Return of Allotment of Shares	1 month
88(3)	Particulars of a contract relating to shares allotted as fully or partly paid up otherwise than in cash	1 month
97	Statement of the amount or rate per cent of any commission payable in connection with the subscription of shares	Before payment
117	Application by a public company for certificate to commence business and Statutory Declaration in support	—
122	Notice of consolidation, division, sub-division, redemption or cancellation of shares or conversion, re-conversion of shares into stock	1 month
123	Notice of increase in nominal capital	15 days
128(1)	Statement of rights attached to allotted shares	1 month
128(3)	Statement of particulars of variation of rights attached to shares	1 month
128(4)	Notice of assignment of name or new name to any class of shares	1 month
129(1)	Statement by a company without share capital of rights attached to newly created class of members	1 month
129(2)	Statement by a company without share capital of particulars of a variation of members' class rights	1 month
129(3)	Notice by a company without share capital of assignment of a name or other designation to a class of members	1 month
139	Application by a public company for re-registration as a private company following a court order reducing capital	15 days or as directed by court

150 COMPANY SECRETARIAL CHECKLISTS

Form No.	Description	Filing period
147	Application by a public company for re-registration as a private company following cancellation of shares and reduction of nominal value of issued capital	15 days
155(6)(a)	Declaration in relation to assistance for the acquisition of shares	15 days
155(6)(b)	Declaration by the directors of a holding company in relation to assistance for the acquisition of shares	15 days
157	Notice of application made to the court for the cancellation of a Special Resolution regarding financial assistance for the acquisition of shares	On notice
169	Return by a company purchasing its own shares	28 days
173	Declaration in relation to the redemption or purchase of shares out of capital	15 days
176	Notice of application to the court for the cancellation of a resolution for the redemption or purchase of shares out of capital	On notice
190	Notice of place where a register of holders of debentures or a duplicate is kept or of any change in that place	On change of address
190(a)	Notice of place for inspection of a register of holders of debentures which is kept in a non-legible form or of any change in that place	On change of address
224	Notice of accounting reference date (to be delivered within nine months of incorporation)	9 months from incorporation
225(1)	Notice of new accounting reference date given during the course of an accounting reference period	During current accounting period
225(2)	Notice of new accounting reference date given after the end of an accounting reference period by a parent or subsidiary undertaking or by a company subject to an administration order	Prior to expiry of period for delivery of accounts for previous year

STATUTORY FORMS AND FILING PERIODS

Form No.	Description	Filing period
244	Notice of claim to extension of period allowed for laying and delivering accounts – overseas business or interest	Before end of accounting period to be extended
266(1)	Notice of intention to carry on business as an investment company	Prior to commencement of investment business
266(3)	Notice that company no longer wishes to be an investment company	On cessation
287	Notice of change in situation of Registered Office	Change takes effect on delivery
288	Notice of change of directors or secretaries or in their particulars	14 days
318	Notice of place where copies of directors' service contracts and any memoranda are kept or of any change in that place	14 days
325	Notice of place where Register of Directors' Interests in shares, etc. is kept or of any change in that place	14 days
325(a)	Notice of place for inspection of Register of Directors' interests in shares, etc. which is kept in a non-legible form or of any change in that place	14 days
353	Notice of place where Register of Members is kept or of any change in that place	14 days
353(a)	Notice of place for inspection of a Register of Members which is kept in a non-legible form or of any change in that place	14 days
362	Notice of place where an overseas branch register is kept, of any change in that place or of discontinuance of any such register	14 days
362(a)	Notice of place for inspection of an overseas branch register which is kept in a non-legible form or of any change in that place	14 days
363(a)	Annual Return of company	28 days

152 COMPANY SECRETARIAL CHECKLISTS

Form No.	Description	Filing period
363(b)	Annual Return of company	28 days
363(s)	Annual Return of company	28 days
386	Notice of passing of resolution removing an auditor	14 days
395	Particulars of mortgage or charge	21 days
397	Particulars for the registration of a charge to secure a series of debentures	21 days
397(a)	Particulars of an issue of secured debentures in a series	21 days
398	Certificate of registration in Scotland or Northern Ireland of a charge comprising property situated there	21 days
400	Particulars of a mortgage or charge subject to which property has been acquired	21 days
401	Register of mortgages and charges	21 days
403(a)	Declaration of satisfaction in full or in part of mortgage or charge	—
403(b)	Declaration that part of the property or undertaking charged (a) has been released from the charge or (b) no longer forms part of the company property or undertaking	—
405(1)	Notice of appointment of receiver or manager	7 days
405(2)	Notice of ceasing to act as receiver or manager	7 days
429(4)	Notice to non-assenting shareholders	7 days
429(dec)	Statutory Declaration relating to a notice to non-assenting shareholders	—
430(A)	Notice to non-assenting shareholders	—
680(a)	Application by a joint stock company for registration under Part XXII of CA 1985 and declaration and related statements	Required for registration
680(b)	Application by a company which is not a joint stock company for registration under Part XXII CA 1985 and declaration and related statements	Required for registration
684	Registration under Part XXII CA 1985 giving list of members in existing joint stock company	Required for registration

STATUTORY FORMS AND FILING PERIODS 153

Form No.	Description	Filing period
685	Application by a joint stock company for registration as a public company; Statutory Declaration that conditions satisfied	Required for registration
686	Registration under Part XXII CA 1985 Statutory Declaration verifying list of members	Required for registration
691	Return and declaration delivered for registration by an overseas company	1 month of establishing in GB
692(1)(a)	Return of alteration in the charter statutes of an overseas company	21 days
692(1)(b)	Return of alteration in the directors or secretary of an overseas company or in their particulars	21 days
692(1)(c)	Return of alteration in the names or addresses of persons resident in Great Britain authorised to accept service on behalf of an overseas company	21 days
692(2)	Return of change in the corporate name of an overseas company	21 days
694(a)	Statement of name other than corporate name under which an overseas company proposes to carry on business in Great Britain	On change of name
695(b)	Statement of name other than corporate name under which an overseas company proposes to carry on business in Great Britain in substitution for name previously registered	On change of name
701(a)	Notice of accounting reference date by an overseas company	As 224
701(b)	Notice by an overseas company of new accounting reference date given during the course of an accounting reference period	As 225(1)
701(c)	Notice by an overseas company of new accounting reference date given after the end of an accounting reference period	As 225(2)

154 COMPANY SECRETARIAL CHECKLISTS

Form No.	Description	Filing period
F 395	Particulars of a mortgage or charge on property in England and Wales created by a company incorporated outside Great Britain	21 days
	Scottish forms	
410	Particulars of a charge created by a company registered in Scotland	21 days
413	Particulars for registration of a charge to secure a series of debentures	21 days
413(a)	Particulars of an issue of debentures out of a series of secured debentures	21 days
416	Particulars of a charge subject to which property has been acquired by a company registered in Scotland	21 days
417	Register of charges, alterations to charges, memoranda of satisfaction and appointments and cessations of receivers	21 days
419(a)	Applications for registration of a memorandum of satisfaction in full or in part of a registered charge	—
419(b)	Application for registration of a memorandum of fact that part of the property charged (a) has been released from the charge or (b) no longer forms part of the company property	—
466	Particulars of an instrument of alteration to a floating charge created by a company registered in Scotland	21 days

Statutory registers

The Companies Act requires the following registers to be kept by all companies:

1. Register of Members.
2. Register of Charges.
3. Minute Books of the proceedings of meetings of the shareholders and its directors and of any sub-committees of the directors.
4. Accounting records.
5. Register of Directors and Secretaries.
6. Register of Directors' Interests and Shares and Debentures.
7. If the company is a public company, Register of Interests in Voting Shares.

Although not required by the Act, if the company maintains a Register of Debenture Holders there are requirements laid down by the Act governing its maintenance and inspection.

The following rules apply to all the company's statutory registers:

1. The Register of Charges together with copies of the instruments creating the charges and the Register of Directors and Secretaries must be kept at the Registered Office.
2. The Register of Members must be kept either at the Registered Office or at some other place within the country of registration. If the Register has not at all times been kept at its Registered Office, the Registrar of Companies must be notified of any change in the place where the Register is kept (form 352).
3. The Register of Directors' Interests and Shares and Debentures must be kept either at the Registered Office or at the place where the Register of Members is kept. If this Register has not at all times been kept in the Registered Office, it will be necessary to inform the Registrar (form 325).

4. The Register of Interests in Voting Shares must be kept at the same place as the Register of Directors' Interests.
5. If a Register of Debenture Holders is kept, it must be kept either at the Registered Office or at some other place within the country of registration. If the Register has not at all times been kept at the Registered Office, the Registrar must be notified (form 190).
6. Copies of the terms of directors' service contracts must be kept at the Registered Office or at some other office within the country of registration. Where these copies have not been kept at the Registered Office, the Registrar must be notified (form 318).
7. The minutes of all the general meetings of the company or of any class meetings must be kept at the company's Registered Office.

Companies House requirements

- Forms G190, G318, G325, G352.

References

The Companies Act 1985 S190, S191, S211, S318, S352–S362 (inclusive), S407–S422 (inclusive).